The Turned-On Couple is outstanding! Corinne offers a path for couples that will keep their partnership and sexuality alive and growing in intimacy. This book is full of helpful advice and real-life experiences that span every challenge couples face in love, passion and pleasure. From diagnosing problem areas to clear directives for renewal, these are all essential lessons every couple needs if they are committed to intimacy for a lifetime.

William R. Stayton, MDiv, ThD, PhD

(Retired) Professor and Director, Human Sexuality Program,

Widener University, Chester, PA

Author of *Sinless Sex*

In *The Turned-On Couple,* Corinne Farago expertly guides couples to explore love and passion. The book contains concise and to-the-point chapters ranging in a broad spectrum of challenges couples face. She blends wisdom, lessons and practical techniques to help long-term couples deepen their connection emotionally and physically.

The Turned-On Couple is serious, fun, and sexy. Corinne blends wisdom, lessons and practical techniques. It's a welcome addition to the ever-growing field of coupledom.

Arthur Colman, M.D. Clinical Professor of Psychiatry. University of California Medical School, S.F. Jungian Analyst.

Author of *Love and Ecstasy* and *Pregnancy: The Psychological Experience.*

It used to be easy – the newness of your relationship kept you passionate, excited, involved, communicative. Now, after years or decades together, the thrill and intimacy have fallen away.

How can you fix it?

In *The Turned-On Couple,* Corinne Farago is your personal sex coach in a book. In short, digestible and actionable nuggets, she offers invaluable advice and strategies for meeting your challenges and enriching every part of your relationship.

Joan Price, Sex Educator, Speaker, Podcaster

Author of *Naked at Our Age* and *Sex After Grief*

Relationship and intimacy coach Corinne Farago takes on "comfortably numb" relationships (predominantly heterosexual), with compassionate wisdom about intimacy, desire, and the many splendors of sex. *The Turned-On Couple* is for the couples who wonder where the magic went. It offers them a comprehensive map for getting it back and reveling in a sexier, deeper connection.

Carol Queen PhD, author of *The Sex & Pleasure Book:*

Good Vibes Guide to Great Sex for Everyone

THE
TURNED-ON
COUPLE

YOUR PATH TO LASTING LOVE, PASSION AND PLEASURE

CORINNE FARAGO

The Turned-On Couple: Your Path to Lasting Love, Passion, and Pleasure

Published by Enlightened Indulgence Press.

ISBN 979-8-9911440-0-1

First Edition
www.corinnefarago.com

Edited by Guy Crittenden
Copyedited by Carol Broderick, Devon Welsh
Book cover by Katarina Naskovski
Layout by Dawn Black
Skillful guidance by Michael LeValley
Unconditional love and support by Jeff Sills

They are one person,
They are two alone,
They are three together,
They are for each other.

— Stephen Stills

Contents

Your First Coaching Tip

Let me guess. When you and your partner got together you hoped to be among the lucky couples who get it right. You hoped that somehow, all the pieces would magically fall into place; communication would flow easily, and sexual fulfillment would last. You hoped your commitment would remain unwavering, and friends and family would forever see you as the *perfect couple*.

If you're reading this, it may be because those hopes are yielding to the challenges that come with the *reality* of long-term love.

Here's my first coaching tip to you both: Don't interpret your current challenges as a sign that you're in the *wrong relationship* with the *wrong person,* or that your relationship is *broken*. Instead, recognize you've entered a new relationship phase in which the challenges simply mean it's time for you and your partner to *learn and grow together*. I'm so happy you have found this book. I wrote it for you.

Here are seven truths you'll learn from reading this book:

1. Moving quickly from conflict back to connection is learnable.

2. Trust and emotional security in a relationship is a prerequisite to great sex.

3. Talking about sex with your partner can be as easy as talking about lunch.

4. Desire isn't a total mystery, and there are many ways to build it (or destroy it).

5. It's perfectly normal to not desire sex that doesn't bring you pleasure.

6. There are ways to heal from feelings of shame and trauma.

7. There is a full spectrum of sexual flavors. Learning and accepting your inherent erotic nature is a core step in your journey.

These are just a few of the truths I wish someone had explained to me decades ago, and they are the very lessons I teach couples today.

Preface

So, what led me to become a relationship and intimacy coach? I discovered the joy of sex when I was still a virgin.

Let me explain.

At thirteen I found a copy of the book *The Joy of Sex* tucked under a shoe box in the top of my mother's closet. For a young girl still fantasizing about kissing boys, the content of this groundbreaking book was eye-opening to say the least. Written at the height of the 1970's sexual revolution, it represented a giant leap into the world of adult sexuality. From my secret afternoon studies of this book, I garnered that sex was an entire world designed for the purpose of giving and receiving pleasure.

I'd spend hours thumbing through the detailed illustrations of naked couples embracing, kissing with open mouths, touching each other's genitals, and pleasuring each other — all the while smiling, sometimes laughing, and (from what I could see) loving each other. What I learned didn't spare me from the challenges that lay ahead, but *The Joy of Sex* introduced me to sex education and coupledom in its most positive light, and served as a beacon of hope that sex and intimacy was not only something which I could look forward to experiencing but, with the right guidance, learn how to do well! And for that I'm truly grateful.

As a teenager, sex sat at the hub of my emotional turbulence, as well as that of my friends who either longed to have it, endlessly sought it, or ran from it in shame and confusion. It became the focal point of our teenage brains; talking about sex and attraction was of great interest to me –the good, the bad, and the ugly of it.

I met my first husband at the young age of nineteen. It wasn't many years before we found ourselves in a low-sex marriage. No one warned us about the trap couples so easily fall into that depletes their desire. In fact, not a word of wisdom was spoken about how to make love, embrace pleasure, or nurture desire in a long-term partnership. With poor initiation skills and no understanding of how seduction works, my young husband and I became stuck in a cycle that left me feeling guilty and pressured, and my husband silently withdrawn and moody. At the time neither of us understood that there is a path through such quagmires of discontent. Like many couples, we lived together more like siblings than lovers. After eight years the marriage ended.

I moved in and out of monogamous relationships, mostly lasting six or more years. Each would begin with deep passion, but ultimately end with some form of sexual or emotional disconnection. From what I could see, long-term relationships were doomed to a fate of boredom, dissatisfaction or infidelity.

I was disheartened and disillusioned by coupledom and its promises of enduring soul-love. In my eyes, the myth of true love stood in stark contrast to the rates of heartbroken breakups and divorces. Why was long-term love and passion so difficult to find and maintain?

In 2007 I moved to San Francisco and decided to finally explore this quandary from a more structured and educated perspective. I put myself back to school, studying, training, and exploring the world of *(you guessed it)* sex and intimacy. I studied couples therapy, somatic sex therapy, hypnotherapy, relationship coaching, and I began to apply that learning to my own life, this time approaching relationships with some tools to tackle the pitfalls of long-term love.

I was grateful to live in a city known for its open embrace of sexual expression and diversity. Trail-blazing sex educators were challenging the status quo. The mindset was sex-positive. Sexual challenges and shame were conditions to be healed, not suffered in silence. The pursuit of pleasure, the demystification of desire, the debunking of outmoded sexual myths were all conversations that were taking place. It was an exciting and liberating time for sex education.

The book that first opened my eyes to the *joy of sex* so many decades ago had planted a seed that now had the fertile ground to flower. I was finding answers to my own questions and quandaries. The pursuit of long-term love and passion that seemed so mysterious now felt attainable, not just for me but anyone with the desire to learn and grow together with their partner.

I opened a private coaching practice in 2010 and since that time have worked with individuals and couples, all of whom were seeking answers to the same questions I struggled with most of my life. For me personally, I came to understand and empathize with my younger self. I was not uniquely broken; nor are the couples I coach uniquely broken. How can we know what we're not taught? Communication challenges, conflict mismanagement, desire discrepancy, and lackluster sex lives are commonplace in long-term relationships.

In my coaching practice, I see all the common pitfalls, and I also see the transformations that come with honest conversations, curiosity, kindness and shared explorations. It's never too late for adult sex and love education!

We're all lifetime students when it comes to sex and intimacy, and every new decade presents more help to those who seek it out.

In these pages, you'll find the fundamental lessons, insights and strategies developed through many years of coaching clients. Their honest, vulnerable and courageous journeys inspired me to write this book.

Most of my coaching couples over the years live in monogamous, heterosexual relationships. Much of this book reflects that fact. However, when I coach same-sex or non-binary couples the same lessons apply. Every couple, regardless of gender identity or sexual orientation, can grow by learning the importance of building and maintaining the emotional intelligence and sexual polarity that builds passion and sustains love.

I am in awe of, and so grateful to the many therapists, researchers and scholars who have informed my coaching practice, and inspired me to focus on the challenges couples face in long-term love and intimacy. They are too many to list here. Their work spans the last four decades. With each decade the field of relationship and intimacy studies has evolved in its scope and wisdom. It is an endlessly fascinating and satisfying world in which to work.

I happily reside in the San Francisco Bay Area with my partner of over 15 years, Jeff, living, loving, and forever learning together.

How To Use This Book

In *The Turned-On Couple,* you'll find **sixty-five concise chapters,** each with an essential, stand-alone lesson designed to inspire you to grow in love and passion with your partner.

Each chapter is a three-to-seven-minute read and serves as a nugget of wisdom and guidance. Allow these lessons to open conversations between you and your partner.

The chapters are divided into three parts that progress from love to sex.

— Book One: **Tune In - Love and Relationships**
— Book Two: **Turn Up - Desire and Initiation**
— Book Three: **Turn On - Sex and Intimacy**

Here are four ways to use this book to inspire change:

1. **If you currently have a partner in your life,** share a chosen (or randomly selected) chapter with them. Read it out loud (3-7 mins) and allow it to guide you both into a conversation that will

enliven and enlighten you as a couple. Set your phone alarm at 15 minutes. Start sharing your thoughts and just see what comes up. In other words, use this book to initiate conversations that will lead to insights and honest sharing.

2. **Read The Turned-On Couple from start to finish** as it progresses through the broad landscape of coupledom. Tune In: Love and Relationships, Turn Up: Desire and Initiation, Turn On: Sex and Intimacy.

3. **Randomly or intuitively open it to any stand-alone chapter** and use it as your "private relationship beacon" for that day or that week. Ponder it. Notice how the topic applies to your relationship. Then experiment with new patterns of behavior with an open mind and a curious heart.

4. **Refer to the content page or the index,** and zero in on a subject that might be pertinent to your relationship currently.

Allow this book to lead you into the nooks and crannies of your partnership and shine some light on the areas that have lingered in the shadows for too long.

BOOK ONE:
TUNE IN

Tune in to yourself and your partner and become a full participant in the growth of your relationship. One of the seven truths of being a turned-on couple is that trust and emotional security is a prerequisite for great sex. If your relationship is strained by resentment, conflict, broken trust, or poor communication, your intimate life will suffer.

In this section you'll learn about the essential skills of building a secure and loving foundation for your intimacy to thrive. Use these lessons to guide you and your partner in conversation, and discover how to build new habits in love that support your passion.

Turned-on couples aren't challenge-free — they're just adept at using the tools they've gathered to grow emotionally and erotically.

1.

The Cold, Hard Truth About Long-Term Relationships: Have You Become "Comfortably Numb"?

There's no dodging the fact that couples in long-term relationships impact one another profoundly, in small and large ways. If you're a couple who lives together, there are moments throughout each day that bring you together to discuss something, to work on a task, to accomplish an errand, and to share (or listen to) a story.

Partners flow in and around each other with such symbiosis that we sometimes feel like we're one mechanism with a shared mind.

The functioning nature of our long-term partnerships becomes hardwired into our brains, just like everything else we do, day-in, day-out. Once we settle into any repetitive pattern, our neurons minimize energy and attention on the subject at hand. It's effective, it's familiar, it's secure, and — in the case of relationships — it's hazardous!

Simply put, *we become numb to our partners.*

This is the cold, hard truth about LTR's (long-term relationships). The good news is this numbing disease isn't terminal. There is a cure, and it's called *awareness*!

Just as we trained our brains to become "comfortably numb," we can train our brains to bring awareness to our daily encounters with our partner. Awareness snaps us out of our slumber of familiarity and reminds us numerous times a day that we can shift out of old patterns and into new ones.

One of my "wake-up" exercises I introduce to *comfortably numb* couples is to bring awareness to their daily interactions with their partner. At the end of an interaction, they can ask themselves, "How would my partner rate the feeling quality of that exchange on a scale of 1 to 10?" (With 1-3 being negative, 5-7 being neutral, and 7-10 being positive.)

No one's keeping score. It's not a game to *win*. It's simply an exercise that brings awareness to our encounters with our partner as they cross our path throughout the course of a day. What rating our partner assigns to our encounters is largely our choice and within our control.

Bringing awareness to our relationship reminds us that we choose how we impact our partner each day. Ask yourself honestly: What kind of general rating would your partner assign to their experience of you on a daily basis? Would they give you a two? A six? A nine?

Do they walk away from you drained by your complaints or energized by your praises? Do you leave them with a furrowed brow of concern, or a smile and a chuckle over a silly joke? Do they get the best of your energy, or do they experience you running on autopilot, putting out as little energy as possible in your exchange?

Ongoing daily encounters in the range of 1-5 are a sign that a relationship is not being enlivened or fueled with the kind of energy that nurtures connection and stimulates intimacy. A 1-5 range relationship dampens our happiness and deadens our enjoyment. If most encounters leave our partners feeling drained, their sense of connection to us will be laced with resentment or avoidance.

If we want our partner to come away from an encounter with us feeling in the 7-10 range, we must bring more awareness to what gets them there. Perhaps their 7-10 range incorporates words that leave them feeling appreciated or cared for. Perhaps it's a look that communicates desire and flirtatiousness, or a touch that says, "I care. I've got your back." Perhaps it's a silly face or a shared joke.

So, what quality of energy do you generally bring to your partner? Even the most mundane daily encounters wire our brains to seek the things that give us pleasure and repel those that give us pain. It's not surprising then, that couples who generally live in the 1-5 range have a harder time accessing the kind of trust and connection that elicits desire in the bedroom. **Fulfilling sex lives are nurtured every day in the small connecting moments we create with our partner *outside* of the bedroom.** Therefore, bring awareness to the energy you bring to your partner daily, and ask yourself, "Did I bring my partner a 1-5 or a 5-10 experience?"

Ultimately, the choice is yours.

2.

Loving in Cruise Control:
How to Shift Your Relationship Back into Manual

You're driving down the freeway, starting out on a multi-hour road trip. At the beginning you must pay attention to a lot of information. The details include where you're headed and easy access to things like water or a snack. You set your preferred temperature. You tune into your favorite podcast or music.

You pay close attention to the road as you move through congested traffic, but once you're on the straight and narrow, you move from the fast lane to the middle, where there's less pressure to pass. You prefer a speed that's within the limit and feels safe. Finally, you shift the car into cruise control. You can sit back, relax and take your mind off the details of driving.

If we're honest with ourselves, we know when we've *put our relationship into cruise control.* In fact, many couples I see feel like they've been in cruise control for years!

We're together with our partner day in and day out. Each week looks the same as the last. The passing scenery isn't changing. We're not even sure of our destination anymore! We just go along, without having much impact on the trip's progression. We've become passive passengers in our relationship, cruising in automatic.

Here and there we notice road signs, urging us to pay attention:

> **Warning**: Loss of sex and intimacy for the next 5 miles (years)!
> **Warning**: Sharp words and impatience around every corner!
> **Warning**: Slippery silences and suppressed emotions ahead!

What are the consequences of no longer trying our best, or just getting lazy behind the wheel? We start ignoring the warning signs that are passing us by.

Here are 18 warning signs that your relationship may be in cruise control:

> You rarely laugh together anymore.
> You brace yourself for expected conflict.
> Disagreements are left unresolved and ignored.
> You stop saying thank you.
> You stop caring about what you look like to your partner.
> You complain more than you praise.
> You stop holding hands or cuddling.
> You hide behind your phone.
> You no longer look for little surprises that would put a smile on your partner's face.
> You stop initiating fun activities together.
> You prioritize other family and friends over your partner.
> You treat your partner like a roommate.
> You use separate bedtimes to avoid intimacy.
> You take your partner's efforts for granted.

The lower-desire partner says no to sex as an ongoing pattern.

The higher-desire partner bargains, withdraws, or gives up trying to initiate.

You avoid conversations about deeper feelings.

Are you nodding your head in recognition as you read this list? If so, it's time to take your relationship out of cruise control and put it back into manual! No one else is going to do it for you.

Put your foot on the peddle and take control of your relationship again by following these six "rules of the road":

1. **Go off-roading**. See some new landscapes and inspiring vistas that take your breath away. Welcome the mystery of the roads less traveled. Get lost and let go of knowing what's coming around the corner.

2. **Interrupt familiar routes**. If you both watch TV every night, do something different. Read a chapter of a good book out loud, massage your partner's shoulders, play a board game; be the one to say, "Hey let's go somewhere special and watch the sun set."

3. **Slow down**. Make time for some deeper conversations; slow down, go for a walk, point out beautiful things around you — a sun-streaked sky, a budding flower, a spider's web. Even amid madness, miracles are all around us.

4. **Speed up**. If your life has been moving at a turtle's pace between the fridge and the couch, put your foot on the gas and pick up the energy! Sing karaoke, dance to your favorite music, listen to some comedy, bring some levity into your partner's life, and pull them away from the news for a few hours.

5. **Drive outside of your comfort zone**. Set a goal together that challenges your skill or endurance. Climb that local cliff, walk that steep trail, extend yourselves beyond what's familiar and easy. Meet challenges together and bond with a shared sense of accomplishment.

6. **Enjoy the ride**. Every night before you go to sleep, name three things you appreciated about your partner that day. Say them out loud. "I appreciated how you dealt with the kids today." Or "I noticed how patient you were when my meeting went late. Thank you for holding me when I felt overwhelmed."

It's time to bring your *full attention* back to the road you're traveling.

Lovers, keep on loving

If you're fortunate enough to have someone special in your life to love, make it your job to be the best partner you can be. Help to ease your partner's burdened mind. Give them the emotional security to contend with the troubles of the world, and help them find refuge where they need it most, in their lover's arms. And if there are parts of your relationship that are less than wonderful, there's a way through.

3.

Your Most Important Threesome: Ten Ways to Nurture Your Relationship Back to Health

You might think that having a threesome would be exciting, but the truth is, you're already in a "threesome." There's you, your partner, *and your relationship*.

When we begin to view our relationship as the third in our threesome, it's easier to see how we are either feeding it with attention and nurturing care or literally ignoring it to death.

It's not uncommon for couples to live busy, high-functioning lives, while the third in their threesome feels depressed and neglected. Have you checked in on your relationship lately? Taken its temperature, observed its skin tone, its energy level, and its mental health? Is it getting the kind of nurturing it needs to grow and deepen? Or is it so bored it's wondering if it's worth the energy to stick around?

The entity we call "relationship" follows us wherever we go. It's in the car on our errands together. It's in the bed with us at night. It's at the breakfast table. And yet, we somehow manage to ignore it, taking for granted that it's going to be there when we finally find the time to engage with it. Our attention is pulled in other directions (like work or family). We're drawn to louder, flashier intruders that make their way into our living rooms like news feeds, social media and entertainment. The world is frantically fighting for our attention, while our relationship sits stoically in the corner of the room feeling defeated and starved.

Ask yourself: If your relationship could sit down and talk with the two of you, what would it have to say? Is it feeling alive and appreciated? Is it having a good time with the two of you?

When a couple begins coaching with me, they usually see that their relationship looks a little frail, because it's not getting the nutrients to grow and thrive. Part of a couple's work together is to nurse their relationship back to health, and learn how to feed it with a daily diet of attention, presence, desire and commitment. For some couples, feeding their relationship might start with as simple a gesture as holding hands when they go for a walk. For others it might be sitting down at the end of their day to check in and share their feelings about things. It might be planning weekly date nights that are more than the usual "same old, same old." Small daily gestures are the most powerful ways to sustain the health and wellness of your relationship.

Here's a new diet to strengthen your relationship, and bring your full attention back to the very important third in your threesome:

> **Take turns creating mystery dates for each other regularly.** Initiate new experiences together. It doesn't have to be expensive or exotic, but when one person takes charge of the date by planning it, preparing for it, and keeping it a secret from the other, it creates anticipation and mystery, and it sets the scene for some focused quality time together (i.e., with your "relationship"). Check out your

local area for some fun activities or grab a basket and a blanket and find a secluded spot to kick back. (And leave your phones in the car!)

Be willing to be happy, rather than be right. There are probably numerous times a day when you could make the choice to be more agreeable when you feel a conflict arising, when you could say something kind and affirming, rather than critical. Look for those moments when the choice is yours to exercise your conciliatory nature and go the extra mile.

Take interest in how your partner feels. Make time each day to check in and show your interest in how your partner is doing. Take your partner by the hand, sit them down, and create the space for them to let go and open up. It sounds simple and maybe obvious, but a busy life can easily suck all our energy, leaving very little left over to say, "Hey, how are you? I care about what's happening in your heart."

Acknowledge your partner when they make an extra effort. When we're generous with our praise and point out the things that make us happy, we affirm that action in our partner, and return the gesture with our appreciation. *If that sounds a bit like dog training, it's because it is!* Couples do behavioral training with each other all the time. Instead of using punishment, fill your pockets with treats. It goes so much further!

Laugh together. Whether it's coming from your naturally keen wit or a favorite standup routine, find ways to laugh out loud together, and counter the seriousness of life that can pull your energy down. Actively look for things that might put a smile on your partner's face. Nominate yourself as the ambassador of humor and regularly feed your relationship some fresh belly laughs.

Get physical. Cuddle, dance, wrestle, make love, massage, learn partner yoga — whatever physical activity brings your bodies together. Use your bodies to connect and bond. Get your limbic systems near each other and let your brain chemistry do its thing. *It's nature's antidepressant.*

Extended hugging. The practice of extended hugging is simple. Once or twice a day, when you come in for a hug, agree to hang onto each other for 20 seconds. You'll get a good hit of oxytocin, your cortisol levels will drop, and you'll remember there's immense refuge to be found in the arms of someone who loves you.

Show desire. It's easier to feel desired than to show desire. How good are you at making your partner feel desired? Do you show your desire, or keep it hidden? Be vulnerable enough to show your desire, flirt, tease, compliment your partner, and show them that you find them attractive. Showing desire doesn't always have to lead to sex. Let desire out to play and enjoy the energy exchange for its own sake.

Talk about sex openly and honestly. When couples learn how to talk about sex from a place of curiosity and playfulness, they realize that sex talk can be fun. Talk about what you like and want more of. Talk about sex after you have sex, and share your highlights. If sex has become boring, you know it's time to start growing again.

Become a student of love. Exercise compassion, empathy, and forgiveness on a regular basis. Even the healthiest relationship has its challenges. Learn to take the higher road. Let go of grudges. Step into your partner's shoes. Be willing to say, "I'm sorry." All these things demonstrate your ability to love. Never stop learning how to love better.

These are just a few items on your relationship's new daily menu. You'll start to see the benefits almost immediately. It will show in the smile on your partner's face when they see you. It'll show in the lack of small conflicts that formerly ate away at intimacy. It'll show in your partner's intimate invitations. It'll show in your partner's look of love from across the table, for no apparent reason.

Before your relationship heads out the door looking for another couple to join up with, sit down as a threesome and assure your relationship that from now on, you're going to listen to its needs, make it feel special, and prioritize time together. Follow this simple diet and ensure your threesome lasts a lifetime!

4.

Filling Your Partner's Love Tank... When They're Running on "Empty"

In a series of articles I wrote during COVID lockdowns under the theme *Tips for Couples in Captivity* I was inspired by my clients' questions and their suggested solutions. What did I hear? Couples wanted to take advantage of at-home time together to focus on their relationship, including everything from ironing out their conflict wrinkles to having better sex and intimacy.

One of my male clients was frustrated that although he felt he'd turned a corner, his new-found loving gestures to his partner weren't reciprocated — at least not as much as he'd hoped. I suggested he think of his partner as having a *love tank* and a *pain tank* with each holding their relationship's positive and negative experiences.

A **love tank** might hold experiences like laughing together, sharing a loving embrace, words of praise, approval and appreciation, passionate erotic connections, tender heart-centered lovemaking, thoughtful gifts, expressing desire, a relaxing massage, focused time together, and so on.

A **pain tank** is where negative experiences are stored, like last night's argument, a snide off-hand remark, a forgotten promise, a day of the silent treatment, a disconnected sexual experience, a loud accusing voice, a betrayal (old or new), or feelings of neglect, for example.

I told him that his partner's hesitancy may be because their love tank was running on empty and, given the recent period of emotional struggles between them, their partner's pain tank was probably quite full. If it's easier to access a full tank of pain than to dip into the love tank of happy memories, patience and understanding might be in short supply. If we feel resentment and resistance more than open heartedness, our love tank likely needs filling (with small consistent gestures) until it's full again. As our love tank gets filled our hearts open (metaphorically and viscerally). Bonding hormones like serotonin and dopamine flood our brains with good feelings. When our love tanks are filled, we have the capacity to extend ourselves and meet our partner's needs. We're moved to give back in return. We feel gratitude, appreciation, and generosity. We feel safe and taken care of by our partner. We feel filled up, as in "My cup runneth over."

Keep that image in mind whenever you spend time with your partner. Ask yourself at the end of each day, "Did I add to my partner's love tank or their pain tank today?" (You'll know the answer by how they're currently behaving towards you.) How patient and generous are *they* these days? Are they extending themselves *toward* you, or armoring themselves *against* you? Are they *welcoming* you when you walk in the door? Or do you feel *invisible* as they run on emotional autopilot?

Let's make a list of offerings that fill our love tank. Here are some ideas that I categorized into Gary Chapman's Love Languages:

Words of Appreciation

- Hearing their words of love and admiration
- Feeling desired and being told you're attractive
- Hearing that your partner's life is better with you in it
- Hearing a "yes" when you're prepared for a "no"
- Being seen and heard in a way that makes you feel understood
- Being forgiven when you know you could have done better

Acts of Service

- Having a favorite meal or dessert prepared for you
- Being relieved of your least favorite chore
- Being encouraged to ask for what you want
- Getting help with a difficult task
- Being treated to a special mystery date

Receiving Gifts

- Receiving surprise gifts for no reason
- Being whisked away on a surprise adventure
- Being treated to a favorite outing
- Having your needs anticipated before you even know what they are

Quality Time

- Going for a walk hand-in-hand or arm-in-arm
- Being listened to like you're the most important person in the world
- Choosing a favorite activity and doing that together
- Dancing and singing together like nobody's watching
- Being granted needed alone time for yourself to do as you wish

Physical Touch

- Enjoying an erotic adventure together
- Getting a massage just the way you like it
- Receiving your favorite sexual delights without asking
- Getting an extended hug out of the blue
- Feeling your partner's arm around you when you need it most
- Making out like a teenager (that means clothes on)

Here's a challenge for you: Make a tailor-made list of things your partner can do to fill up your love tank. Then ask your partner to make their own list. Sit down and share your lists with each other. Find out what they think would fill their love tank. You may be surprised at some of your partner's preferences! Keep your partner's list somewhere you can see it often (e.g., a bulletin board or the door of your fridge, or inside your bathroom cabinet). Make a regular daily deposit into their love tank with small consistent gestures. When the tank feels abundant and full, the next time they need reserves they can draw upon it for any extra patience or generosity needed in that moment. And remember to ask yourself (daily and also in *every interaction*), "Did I just add to my partner's love tank? Or did I add to their pain tank?" Keep your beloved partner running on full and the road you travel together will be blessed with warm breezes, free of unwelcome detours.

5.

Feelings... Woah-oh-oh Feelings...
Learning to Identify and Express Them

Once again, I'm inspired to write about a topic raised by more than a few of my coaching clients: the "F" word. The word that makes some of us open up, wanting more, and makes others close down, running in the opposite direction. The word is "feelings."

> ♪♪   ♪♪   "Feelings, nothing more than feelings,
> trying to forget my feelings of love..."   ♪♪   ♪♪

If you know this song, you're probably over fifty. I remember listening to this song on the radio as a teen. They played it endlessly until we were all parodying it. Back then I thought it was pretty sappy, but Albert Morris was a man brave enough to sing about lost love, tears rolling down his face, and his feelings.

This is a time of feelings. We've all been driven deep into our feelings about the world at large, politics, uncertainty, domestic tension, but sharing our feelings with each other is not always easy depending on our upbringing. I'm going to generalize about genders here and preface matters by saying I don't like gender clichés, but I also hear many of my female clients over the years repeat the same frustration with their male partners, so let's talk about it.

Men in our society are not raised to talk about their feelings. But that doesn't mean they don't have them. We're all human beings and have feelings. The difference in genders has a lot to do with how we're raised. When a little girl falls and scrapes her knee, she's comforted, and allowed to cry; she's held and receives sympathy. She's encouraged to express her feelings in the safety of an accepting caregiver.

But when a little boy hurts himself, it's all, "Come on son! Get up! Shake it off! No need for tears. It's hardly a scratch!" from the adults around them. And their peers support that with calling names like "sissy" and "baby." What we're saying to that little boy is, in fact, that their feelings are *wrong*. They're overacting and being too dramatic. What they hear is that their feelings are best kept hidden for fear of being ridiculed and shamed.

This is where the shaming begins, and it continues throughout every part of a boy's life. We want our boys to be strong, but we make the horrible mistake of associating the suppression of feelings with strength and the display of vulnerability with weakness. We set up our boys to grow into men who are unable to access their feelings. Their emotional intelligence is stunted because of our cultural discomfort with male vulnerability.

Women are trained to express their feelings. We huddle in the playground to talk about boys, we pour our feelings into our diaries, and we watch our mothers chat with their friends for hours. We learn how to be vulnerable even when it's uncomfortable for fear of being shunned in our sharing circles. We learn to hold space for sad friends. It's safe for us to cry over a movie or a heartbreak.

When we bring these alternatively trained, emotionally-suppressed men into relationships with women trained differently, the massive disconnect can lead to frustration, misunderstandings and relationship breakups. Women enter a relationship looking for the kind of emotional sharing they got from their female friends; men come in with a desire to be seen as a strong and reliable protector (who won't fall to pieces if he falls down and scrapes his knee). Emotional suppression leads to relationship problems, and often to depression (recognized now as unexpressed feelings of sadness).

Is it any wonder that our world is filled with violence in and out of the home?

It's not the fault of the boys or the men they grow up to be. Relationships create an opportunity for healing to occur, when couples learn to bridge the *feelings gap* between men and women.

Practical solutions

What I'm going to suggest can be applied to any emotional disconnect regardless of gender. If you're going to invite your partner to open up and talk about their feelings, it behooves you to create a safe place for them to do that. By safety I mean a conversational space where they can trust that they won't be shut down, belittled, criticized, made light of or talked out of what they're feeling.

You can lay the ground rules for sharing feelings:

- Feelings are not accusations, finger pointing, or blaming.
- Your feelings are your responsibility.
- Your feelings are about you, not anyone else.
- No one can "make" you feel a certain way.
- Feelings are inherently vulnerable.

Angry feelings are always an overlay for a feeling that's harder to express and a need that's not being met. Dig deeper.

For your partner to share their feelings, they need to trust that it's safe to do so, and trust isn't built in one conversation. It's built over time with many little experiences in which their feelings are welcomed. Feelings are not a flat tire, or anything broken that needs to be fixed. If you're listening to your partner share their feelings and all the while you're thinking about how you can fix it (so they no longer have to experience those feelings), you're missing the opportunity to build trust. Feelings are real and true to the person feeling them, no matter what.

These approaches will diminish trust:

- You jump in with your *own story* about having those feelings.
- You secretly discount the impact of those feelings on your partner.
- You build an argument to defend yourself or counter your partner's feelings with your own.
- You use your partner's confessions against them in the future, thereby confirming that it's not safe to be honest.
- You criticize your partner for *not* sharing their feelings, thereby *training them* to avoid the topic.

Building trust with your partner in a way that makes them safe in the feelings department is actually quite simple. It mostly requires *listening until they're done*, and offering empathetic statements, like "It must be hard to feel that," "I understand what you're saying and why you'd feel that way."

That's it!

Give them the time it takes them to express what they want to say. If you're not sure if more needs to be said, you can ask, "Is there anything else you'd like to say about that?" And then wait.

Sometimes a patient, sympathetic question can open another door for your partner to explore. If the conversation ends with "I think that's all I need to say about that" then you know it's ok to change the subject and honor that they've met their capacity in that moment. Let them hear your appreciation and acceptance.

"Thank you for sharing all that," is a useful phrase that translates as, "I love you. I respect you."

By seeing the positive results of their efforts, your partner will begin to associate the sharing of feelings with the reward of *appreciation* rather than *ridicule* and *shaming*. Fixes, shared experiences, helpful suggestions can all come later. For now, you've met your partner's feelings with respect, and you've helped build more trust that their feelings are safe with you in the future.

In conclusion, create the time and space for your partner's soft vulnerable feelings such as fear, sadness, or grief; allow them to express their feelings before they become hardened expressions of anger, depression, and withdrawal. Behind every man (and woman) raised to become the "strong silent type" there's a small boy (or girl) who believes that being vulnerable is weak and dangerous.

♫♫ ♫♫ "Feelings... Woah-oh-oh Feelings... Woah-oh-oh feelings... again in my heart..." ♫♫ ♫♫

6.

Intimacy in Analog:
Three Simple Steps to Take Your Power Back
from Their Phone

It's hard to believe we've only been living with "smart" phones with internet access since 2007. Prior to that, if couples wanted to ignore each other, they hid behind newspapers.

The old cliché of the man sitting at the dinner table with a newspaper up to his face has been replaced with the couple sitting in a restaurant scrolling their cell phones.

Same problem, same complaint, and same solution, ultimately.

If you're using your phone to avoid human intimacy, connection and conversation, then it doesn't matter what you're hiding behind; you're still hiding. Newspapers had a limited number of pages, with limited stories. At some point you were going to read the whole thing and eventually put it down. But phones connect us to a never-ending universe of information.

Phones have become our *external brain*. There's no end to the thoughts, stories, information, and propaganda our external brain insists on sharing with us, whether we want to hear it in the moment, or not.

We've been well trained to answer the call of our pocket masters. Our brains are now wired to respond to notifications, dings, and bells and their attendant hits of dopamine or cortisol. For most of us, our phones are calling the shots.

A quick look down at our external brain, and there's a whole world of messages and images that say, "Look at me! I'm far more interesting than the human sitting across from you!"

The couples I coach who are over sixty generally have a more utilitarian relationship with their phones. For them, it's about actually having phone calls with human voices on the other end. But for the under sixties — especially those under forty — phone dependency is now on the list of common partner complaints.

A study published in the journal *Psychology of Popular Media Culture* examined how smartphone use and smartphone dependency affect the health of relationships among college-aged adults. The study showed a significant correlation between higher levels of dependency on smartphones and higher levels of relationship uncertainty.

Think about this: the typical American checks their smartphone once every six-and-a-half minutes, or roughly one hundred and fifty times a day. How many of these phone checks pause an intimate conversation with a loved one or interrupt some other shared moment of human connection? The affected partner can become trained as well — trained to feel less important, unseen, or discounted by their partner's phone habits. Studies have recently tied phone dependency to partner depression and relationship dissatisfaction.

"She never puts her phone down. Literally."

"Whenever we fight, he goes to his phone and doesn't want to talk."

When I suggest some new etiquette around phone use, it's usually met with a stunned silence. Some couples will look at me like I'm suggesting something quite radical, even dangerous.

I think it's a heroic demonstration of love, to say to your partner, "Let's agree to leave our phones outside of the bedroom," or "Let's leave our phones in the car while we eat out," or "Let's avoid pulling our phones out if we've having a disagreement."

You can even make this formal. Write agreements down and sign your names at the bottom. Get a witness to sign off on it! Do whatever it takes for you both to acknowledge that *agreements have been made,* and then see what happens. Get curious about what life is like when you take your power back from your phones!

What would it be like to remove your "alternate universe" from your together time with your partner and engage in full sentences that have awkward moments of silence, rambling unedited thoughts and even — God forbid — *boredom*. Who knows where it will lead?

It's unfair to ask our partner to compete with the instant gratification of likes, alerts, calls to action, and feeds custom-designed to target our latest AI-monitored interests. By removing our phones from our intimate life, we make the time and space to slow down and explore human connection that goes deeper than our usual day-to-day engagement with our partner. We have the dedicated, uninterrupted time to share ourselves, find out new things about our partner, and stay current with their thoughts, their vulnerability and their intimate confessions.

Every time my phone dings or buzzes with a notification I think about the scene from the Netflix documentary *The Social Dilemma* in which three men are depicted as the controllers behind the phone, working day and night to find ways to draw my attention to my device: texts from friends, social media, Facebook Messenger, news alerts, traffic updates, voicemails.

The Social Dilemma helped me recognize the nonstop war playing out between my phone and my increasingly weary and divided attention. Sometimes I feel like I'm losing the battle, but I'm also hopeful that as we contend with the ongoing invasion of technology into our lives, we will re-define our values and our boundaries.

I hear parents talk about creating restrictions on their kid's phone time, taking their phones away at bedtime or limiting screen time, for example. So, let's bring that same wisdom to protecting our intimate time with our partners.

Here are three simple steps to start taking your power back from your phone:

Acknowledge there's a problem. Listen to your partner. If their experience of your phone use is causing them to feel unimportant it's time to have an honest conversation about phone dependency and solutions.

Agree on priorities. We all have obligations, work commitments, and parental responsibilities, but you can still eliminate the distraction. Set your phone to only allow calls from these important contacts when on "do not disturb," and then use it. The rest can wait.

Create phone-free periods. Agree on specific times when phones are put away in the other room, like while on intimacy dates, after a certain hour in the evenings, during long walks, and while spending time with the kids. For the ambitiously advanced radicals out there, try a techno cleanse for a weekend or a vacation. Give your brain a break from dopamine/cortisol concoctions that come with every notification. Step back into a relaxed world of analog intimacy, extended eye contact, empathetic listening, and conversations that are more than 280 characters.

7.

Vulnerability:
The Prerequisite to Intimacy

> *"Vulnerability is the core, the heart,*
> *the center of the human experience."*
>
> — Brene Brown

My coaching couples lead busy lives; most juggle their schedules to find time to be alone and intimate together. They're effective in getting things done, building careers, organizing kids, and planning life, but somehow this doesn't translate into *vulnerability*, which can't be slotted into a busy day or simply added to a "to-do" list. There's more to it than running a meeting or throwing a dinner party.

When couples come to see me about love and intimacy, they sit down to have one of the bravest conversations they can have as a couple. I appreciate how challenging it is to hear our partner's dissatisfaction or unmet desires. We're not comfortable hearing about our partner's pain. Rather than listening with a desire to understand, we might want to bypass the hard stuff and move directly into "fixing" and "solving."

We hold tight onto our armor and use whatever strategies we've developed to deflect (what feel like) arrows coming our way. Anger, blame, judgment, withdrawal — are all strategies we use to fend off what we fear the most: becoming vulnerable and laying down our shields.

Vulnerability is reached when we dig down below emotions like anger, blame, judgment, and any other reaction that protects our position of victimhood. When we're vulnerable we take ownership of our feelings and accept responsibility for our reactions to life. Vulnerability is a gift that descends upon us when we stop pretending to have it all together and admit to our human flaws and fragility. It's a gift we give to ourselves and our partner, because it shifts our state from one of closed-off superficiality, to one of feeling and deep sharing.

When one partner in a couple opens the door to vulnerability, they create space for their partner to join them there, and it's in that space of shared vulnerability that hearts connect and intimacy is experienced. Vulnerability is a prerequisite to love, intimacy and connected sex. Without it, our relationships skim the surface and stagnate.

Vulnerability and trust

Before we allow ourselves to become vulnerable, we first need to trust that our partner will attune to our feelings and help us feel safe. There are ways to support your partner in their vulnerability:

- Talk less and listen more to what our partner is expressing.
- Not try to fix them or solve their problem in the moment.
- Ask open-ended questions to help them express themselves fully.
- Be judgment free, even if you don't share their perspective.
- Empathize with words or body language of support.
- Accept that they have a right to feel what they're feeling.

Every time we show up for our partner in their vulnerable moments, trust is built. Our partner learns from experience that it's safe to be vulnerable with us, that they'll be heard, and that their truth will be honored.

Vulnerability is sexy. When we open up sexually and let our partner not only into our bodies, but into our hearts, fears, desires, insecurities, we build real intimacy. We also build real intimacy when we risk asking for what we want, take the chance of being seen as less than perfect or let ourselves go into orgasmic pleasure. In our vulnerability we experience the kind of sexual intimacy that's rarely represented in porn or media. Vulnerability is the foundation to great, mind-blowing sex. That's a fact!

If a couple loses their ability to be vulnerable with each other, sex becomes functional or transactional. We go through the motions, feeling disconnected, unmet, and emotionally unfulfilled. Disconnected sex leads to loss of interest and desire, which is the number one reason most couples seek out sex and intimacy coaching. Here are some of the approaches my couples have found helpful in supporting vulnerability:

- Share about your day from a *feeling* rather than a *doing* perspective.
- Practice *radical honesty* from a place of love.
- Admit when you've *made a mistake.*
- Ask for what you want simply and *clearly.*
- Confess disappointment without *blaming.*
- Experiment with keeping your *eyes open* during sex or making out.
- Show your vulnerable feelings. Don't be afraid to *cry.*
- Be curious about your *partner's* experience.
- Ask questions that lead to *vulnerable conversations.*

If we think of our relationship as a garden, imagine vulnerability as one of the ingredients needed to keep your plants growing strong and bearing fruit. Tend to your garden daily with deep watering that sinks down into the roots. Deep feelings and deep sharing will nurture deep love and desire.

8.

I Don't Want to Talk About It: The Yin and Yang of Challenging Conversations

Having coached many couples over the years I hope I've earned the right to make a few broad generalizations based on my exposure to many relationships. For my purpose here, I'll stick with woman/man pronouns.

Consider these two statements:

> Men don't want to talk about their feelings.

> Women don't want to talk about sex.

What an interesting conundrum. Let's look at how this might play out. Here's a client's account of a conversation they had with their partner that illustrates this dynamic. (Beneath every statement is a "thought bubble" that reveals what was hidden behind the words.) Does this exchange sound familiar to you?

Her: How are you doing?

What is he thinking? Why does he feel distant? I wish he'd talk to me.

Him: I'm good. (pause) Why?

(suspicious) What does she want? What am I doing wrong?

Her: Just checking in. I was feeling a little disconnected from you today.

Why is he getting defensive? Can't I ask a simple question?

Him: I've spent the whole day with you. I don't understand what you need from me right now.

I'll never be enough for her. She wants too much.

Her: (frustration) I'm just saying, I want to feel close to you.

I knew something was wrong. Is he mad at me?

Him: Well, I'm not feeling much affection coming from your end either. We haven't had sex in three weeks.

There, I said it! How can she want me to open up, when she never opens up to me.

Her: Is that all you ever think about? I'm not talking about sex right now.

Sex is the only thing that matters to him.

Him: You never want to talk about sex.

I'm not going to share my feelings with someone who doesn't want to have sex with me.

Her: *(in resignation)* Never mind.

I'm not going to have sex with someone who doesn't want to share his feelings with me.

Most of us have had conversations like this one at some point. You both want to feel more intimate, but you're traveling down two different roads trying to get there. He's on the physical road, and she's on the emotional road. Two truths in our society contribute to this confusing conundrum:

1. Boys are raised to keep their feelings to themselves. They're encouraged to internalize their more vulnerable emotions for fear of not appearing strong. If they cry on the playground, it's a sign of weakness. If they open up about their fears, their peers may shame them. If boys aren't taught how to talk about their feelings, conversations about feelings become foreign territory.

2. Girls are raised to say no to sex. Girls are taught that sex can be dangerous. They're warned about getting pregnant or acquiring STDs. If they're a "yes to sex" type they might be labeled as a slut or be sexualized and used by men. By the time girls reach the age of becoming sexual, they've been indoctrinated into suppressing their sexuality.

Ergo, boys grow into men who aren't comfortable talking about their feelings, and girls grow into women who don't feel comfortable talking about sex. So, what do we all need in order to engage with challenging conversations about feelings and sex? We need to feel safe to express *what's true for us*. In order to feel safe being honest, we need to feel safe from judgment and reactivity. If a man finds it challenging to open up about his feelings, he'll look for signs that he's safe. Some of those safety signs might be that his partner

- doesn't criticize or downplay his feelings;
- listens attentively and empathetically;
- accepts that it's not easy for him to open up;
- doesn't try to fix his problem or offer solutions; and
- offers an *invitation* to share, rather than demand to talk.

If a woman finds it challenging to open up about sex, she'll seek signs that it's safe to do so. Some of those signs might be that her partner

- expresses curiosity about her thoughts on sex, rather than blame or judgment;
- hears what she wants without withdrawing or feeling criticized;
- accepts their sexual differences, and is optimistic about finding common ground;
- doesn't attach a conversation about sex to an expectation that it'll lead to sex; and
- guides with open-ended questions about sex while practicing patience and respect.

Ask yourself: How comfortable do you make it for your partner to open up and share themselves in conversations they find challenging? We all have room for improvement, and it's never too late to start creating new patterns of communication based on honesty, acceptance and trust. Yes, men and women are different, but the beauty is found in the interplay of those differences. Just as the ancient Yin-yang symbol illustrates, seemingly opposing differences unite to create a perfect symbiosis of balance and polarity.

Here's the simplest, most concise way I can muster to explain the symbiotic flow of intimacy in the masculine/feminine dynamic:

- When a man shares his more vulnerable feelings, a woman feels connected to him emotionally.
- When a woman feels emotionally attuned to her partner, she's able to let go and connect to her own desire and arousal.
- When a man feels his partner's desire and arousal, he feels connected to his erotic confidence and sexual mastery.
- When a woman feels her partner's erotic confidence, her desire for him deepens.

- When a man feels confident and desired by his partner, he feels emotionally bonded to her and therefore safe to share himself more openly.

And around we go in this beautiful cause-and-effect dance of sex and intimacy. Women want to emotionally connect in order to feel their desire. Men want to feel desired in order to emotionally connect. In conclusion, when a couple learns to embrace challenging conversations and acknowledge their differences, they learn to bend in their partner's direction. This helps them meet each other's needs by recognizing the interplay of opposites that combine to create sex and intimacy.

9.

Old Wounds:
Steps to Heal Wounds and Deepen Intimacy

No matter how well we were parented, cared for, and protected, every one of us grew into adulthood carrying emotional wounds that caused us to form negative beliefs about ourselves and the world around us. (Read that sentence again!) Some of us were wounded in our family home; others were wounded (intentionally) by bullies on the playground, or wounded (unintentionally) by friends. Our trust may have been broken, or our self-confidence undermined.

Life is full of wounding experiences, and some of them leave indelible marks on our heart and psyche that continue to undermine our lives and relationships.

For many of us, this translates into insecurity about our *competence* and *abilities*. Maybe someone told us we weren't good enough or made fun of our skillset as we worked at a task like creating art, or solving a math problem, running a race, or even sharing a joke. We may have felt unpopular and wondered if we were even likable. Many people have a negative view of their bodies. We're unsure if we're physically desirable, or if our bodies work the same as those of other people. And then we get to our sexual preferences and wonder if our ideas are "acceptable" or "normal."

In other words, are we enough just as we are in order to be accepted and loved?

When two people form a relationship, two sets of wounds merge and intertwine — two sets of well-worn, entrenched wounds every couple will have to contend with if they're going to form a lasting, loving, relationship. These combined wounds will inevitably play a lead role in our arguments. Our wounds will be exposed, poked at, and prodded at times by the very people we trust the most.

We know when old wounds are being dragged into a conflict because our pain and defensiveness suddenly spikes. If our partner speaks the same words or speaks in the same tone as our *inner abuser*, the armor will go up, and disagreements may escalate into shouting, tearful battles. The negative stories that arise in such times can be reduced to two universal beliefs: "I'm not good enough" and "You don't love me." Relationship partners have the power to hurt one another by opening old wounds; they also have the power to heal by tending to those wounds.

Here are three things you can practice to gain insight into your partner's wounds and initiate a healing process:

1. Sit down together when you're both feeling calm and talk about which old wounds hold you back in love and life. Ask your partner to share the story behind one of their early wounds. What happened? How did it make them feel?

When old wounds are activated, you may feel

- disrespected,
- alone and lonely,
- excluded,
- judged and misunderstood,
- bullied,

- abandoned,
- attacked and afraid, and/or
- guilty and regretful.

What is the negative inner dialogue or belief that comes from that incident?

- *I can't trust anyone to be there for me.*
- *I'm not smart enough.*
- *I'm not attractive enough.*
- *The world is not a safe place.*
- *People will hurt me or leave me.*
- *I'm not worthy of love.*

Remember, most of our deepest inner wounds were experienced when we were young. They don't necessarily make sense today. The negative story could even sound silly or embarrassing to admit. By speaking our stories out loud, and confessing the origin of our wounds, we help to objectify them and see them for what they are: old stories and beliefs that no longer protect or serve us.

2. Ask your partner to consider how these wounded beliefs get triggered in your present day conflicts. Ask questions that help your partner gain insight into their emotional triggers that stem from old wounds. By better understanding the fears and needs of our partner's younger self, we can avoid poking their wounds and escalating disagreements.

3. Make an agreement to help heal each other's wounds with words and actions that serve as a healing balm. What can you do as loving partners to help each other rewrite that old story? You can help your partner rewrite their old, negative stories by using words and phrases that counter their beliefs. The more you understand the nature of your partner's wounds, the more specific you can be when delivering the right words and phrases to counter their inner dialogue and heal the pain from past events.

Here are some general themes and phrases to give you ideas about helpful things to say:

When they feel insecure about their competence:

> "I know you can do it."
> "I admire so many of your skills."
> "I love how capable you are."

When they're insecure about their body:

> "You look beautiful tonight."
> "You're perfect to me, just the way you are."
> "I'm so attracted to you."

When they're insecure about their identity or personality:

> "I respect your values."
> "You don't have to be like anyone else. You're perfect right now."
> "You're so funny. I love your sense of humor."

When they're insecure about abandonment during conflict:

> "I'll never threaten to leave the relationship in a heated moment."
> "I'm taking a time-out, but I'll be back in 30 minutes to connect and talk."
> "Even if we disagree about something, you come first in my life."

Supportive phrases that build our partner up can get lost in our busy day-to-day lives together. Don't assume your partner doesn't need to hear words that soothe their insecurities. This is *love in action* — the sacred potential and purpose of every intimate relationship.

10.

The Four Levels of Conversation: A Guide to Effective Communication in Relationships

Conversations in a couple's life together range from the mundane to the profound. One moment we need to talk about who's taking the kids to school; the next we might feel the urge to share our deepest fears and longings.

There's a time and place for all of it.

Wouldn't it be exhausting if every conversation with our partner was about processing feelings and deeply probing our emotions? It would be equally unsatisfying for every conversation to skim the surface of life, focusing only on practicalities and tasks. The ability to identify different levels of conversation can help couples communicate more effectively. You can become more *intentional* about what level of conversation is needed in the moment and how to respond to it. This can help you communicate more clearly, set expectations for that conversation, and avoid misunderstandings (which can lead to conflict).

Labeling levels of conversation can provide an easy way for you to communicate your intentions when communicating with your partner. You can use the short forms Level 1, 2, 3, and 4. Let's look at the differences in these levels and how they can help you and your partner identify each other's expectations and needs when initiating a talk.

Defining the four levels of conversation

Level 1: Small Talk and Its Role in Daily Life: This is the most superficial level of conversation, where couples engage in light and easy conversation about everyday topics such as the weather, current events, or work and family schedules. Many of us fill our days with Level 1 conversations. We need them to handle daily life and coordinate with our partner. Usually, our engagement in these conversations leans toward *rational* and *observational*. They're generally *emotionally neutral* and *goal oriented*.

> *Example*: "Sweetheart, after you pick Trevor up from soccer practice, can you pick up some paper towels on the way home? We're almost out. Is there anything else we're needing?"

Level 2: Opinions and How They Deepen Emotional Connection: At this level, we share more personal information and opinions about topics such as our hobbies, interests, and beliefs. We may also discuss current issues that are important to us or debate different perspectives on various topics. Level 2 conversations can deepen emotional connection. They usually involve more personal topics where partners reveal themselves to each other.

We come to understand our partner's feelings and learn more about things that matter to them. We learn about their background such as family memories, fun activities, past challenges, and experiences that contributed to who they are today. By moving beyond superficial small talk and sharing more personal aspects of ourselves, couples can share their experiences and develop a deeper emotional connection. Level 2 conversations help build trust and strengthen the bond between partners.

Example: "I enjoyed helping the kids build that model plane last night. I'd forgotten how much I appreciated the times my dad did that with me. We once assembled a World War Two fighter plane that actually flew!"

Level 3: Dreams and Aspirations for a Stronger Bond: Level 3 conversations are defined by a deeper emotional revelation, often including unedited sharing based on trust, safety, and vulnerability. In the more profound levels of conversation, couples share their ultimate goals and aspirations for their life together. Here we talk about feelings, what's important to us, what excites us and why; we openly share our fears, disappointments, and insecurities.

Example: "I've never told anyone this before but..."

Or

"What I really want you to know about me is..."

These conversations can include subjects likes, beliefs, values, faith, and shared dreams. They create a strong sense of unity and support in the relationship, as well as build a shared sense of meaning and purpose. By discussing our dreams and our doubts we learn to be more honest about who we are and trust that our partner has our back, no matter what.

Level 4: Presence and Being Transparent in the Moment: Level 4 conversation requires us to be even more open and transparent. It's less about conceptualizing, explaining, or dreaming. Level 4 is about presence. It's about noticing and being with what's happening in the moment we're together.

Example: "Right now I feel peaceful/ excited/nervous/relieved."

"I'm feeling grateful for..."

"I'm scared to say this, but... when you expressed your desire just now, I felt insecure about..."

We want to trust that whatever we express will be met with compassion and understanding. When we share our present-time thoughts and feelings, we're letting our partner into our inner world inthat moment. In a relaxed and trusting state, partners can flow with what's presently arising and follow that, wherever it leads.

Level 4 makes room for moments of silence beyond words. It allows our partner to see us as we are, for who we are, with all our imperfections and emotional complexity. There's trust that whatever arises in the present moment is welcome and accepted.

Each level has its time and place. If we're always in Level 3, talking about feelings, we can become weighed down with the emotional processing that deep sharing requires. If we're always in Level 1 conversations, we can slip into autopilot, talking about tasks, kids, work, news, and so on. We end up feeling drained by superficiality and unfulfilled in our desire to be seen and felt on a deeper level.

Identify what level of conversation is best suited for the moment. Use your words to handle the practicalities of life and look for the opportunities to engage in conversations that nurture connection and reveal more of who you are.

Also, learn to step out of your conversational comfort zone. If you avoid some levels of conversation, ask yourself why. Does it feel risky? What are your fears? What patterns of conversation have you and your partner fallen into? Do you assume there's nothing new to learn about your partner? Have you lost the trust you need in order to go deeper?

If you grew up in a family that avoided deep conversations, you might find yourself always gravitating to Level 1. If you were taught that being vulnerable and sharing your emotions is a sign of weakness, you may even fear ridicule or judgment if you open up to your partner. Stay with it. When it comes to learning how to effectively communicate and deepen your connection with another human being, your relationship is your greatest teacher.

If you feel emotionally disconnected from your partner and you want to initiate levels 3 or 4, set aside time for those conversations.

- Ask questions that show interest in your partner's thoughts and experiences.
- Gently lead them with questions that will open them to sharing what's meaningful to them.
- Stay clear of judgments or telling them what to feel.
- Give them time to express themselves fully without trying to fix their problem for them.

Communication strategies for couples

Here are some prompts you can use when exploring these deeper conversations:

"How are you feeling?"
"What do you need right now in order to relax?"
"Are there parts of yourself that are in conflict right now?"
"What's on your mind these days?"
"What are you looking forward to?"

"Tell me the story about..."
"Talk to me, I'm listening."

"Tell me more about that."

"Tell me how you feel about..."

Learn to express tolerance, empathy, and understanding:

"I can see how you would feel that way."

"That must be hard."

"I admire your position on that."

"Let me repeat what I heard you say just now, so I understand."

Get curious! Remember what it was like when you were first becoming acquainted with your partner. There are many things you have yet to discover if you know how to engage your curiosity. Your partner is always changing and growing. *Stay current with who they are today.*

From the mundane to the profound, couples need to navigate through a multitude of conversations. By understanding the four levels of conversations, we get clear on the purpose and intention behind our words. By sharing this common language, couples can set expectations for a conversation, identify the source of conversational frustrations, and express their need for deeper sharing.

11.

Criticism: It's You, Not Me!
How to Identify and Avoid Criticism in
Relationships

Renowned psychologists, John and Julie Gottman have made significant contributions to the field of couples therapy and relationship research. Together, they developed the model known as "The Four Horsemen of the Apocalypse" to describe communication patterns that can predict the end of a relationship. They are:

- **Criticism**
- **Contempt**
- **Stonewalling**
- **Defensiveness**

The Gottmans' findings are based on studies of thousands of couples. Statistics speak volumes when it comes to relationships so let's dive into the First Horseman: Criticism.

Safety is a fundamental requirement in building healthy relationships. We want to feel our partner has our back, understands, supports, and wants the best for us. We hope for trust, communication, generosity, cooperation, sexuality, affection, attention, and humor – all of which require that we feel *safe* with our partner (emotionally, physically, and spiritually). However, when a couple allows criticism to seep into their communication, they can become domestic adversaries either bracing for the next painful exchange or healing from yesterday's wounds.

Identifying signs of criticism

Criticism is not *complaining*. We can complain about a situation; we can complain about something we'd like to change. Complaining turns to *criticism* when we blame our partner for our troubles, more specifically, when we blame and label our partner's *personal traits* as being *wrong* or *bad*.

Here's an example of a simple complaint that rolls into criticism.

Nora: "Adam, you forgot to take out the trash in time for garbage day again." Adam: "Yup, I missed this week."

Nora: "You're so forgetful and lazy. You never remember to do anything around the house!"

Adam: "You're a nag. You obsess about all the things I do wrong. You never appreciate anything I do around here."

Their communication about the trash escalated quickly from facts to criticism and ended in anger. The issue of the trash wasn't resolved with an agreement of how to avoid missing garbage day again, but went straight to accusations leaving them both feeling hurt and defensive. This pattern of criticism will erode an emotional connection and threaten a relationship over time.

If you're triggered and your statements start with words like, "You always...", or "You never...", then you're resorting to criticism. If you label your partner using negative words like lazy, irresponsible, stupid, flaky, hysterical, or controlling, you're resorting to criticism.

If a person regularly hears negative comments attacking their character, it will affect their self-worth, which can lead to resentment, anger and contempt. They'll feel attacked, judged, and insecure in the relationship, provoking them to either fight back with their own criticism or withdraw emotionally from the relationship. Ongoing criticism lowers their overall self-esteem and increases defensiveness, making communication and problem-solving difficult. This cycle of negativity inevitably ends with the criticized person feeling *attacked* and the criticizer feeling *unheard*.

Stepping out of this escalation takes some skill and awareness. Most of all, it requires practice.

Two steps to end critical conflict:

1. Lay Down Your Weapons

Make an agreement with your partner that if either of you catch criticism being used as a weapon in your disagreements, one or both of you can call it out and lay your weapons down. Take some steps to back out of the battle and shift to a more constructive way of expressing your frustration.

If emotions are ramped up, de-escalate by calling for a "time-out" until you feel calmer. Taking a time-out doesn't mean sweeping it under the rug and never talking about it again, however. Agree on how much time you both need. Maybe that's five minutes? Or an hour? If you call for the time-out, you need to be the person who comes back and moves the conversation forward.

Start with what you're feeling (e.g., confused, lonely, sad, frustrated). Name it and don't blame your partner for making you feel that way. Use

"I" statements rather than assigning blame. Take turns identifying the need your partner has that's not being met in this situation. Don't assume you're getting it right. Ask them and listen until you *do* get it right. You must each take responsibility for contributing to the escalation. Most importantly, agree on an action you can both take going forward to avoid repeating the same conflict. Get on the same team to solve the problem and find solutions before the conversation ends.

2. Nip It in The Bud

Once you get good at identifying the signs of criticism, you can nip it in the bud before it builds into a battle. Did the critical words already leave your mouth? Ask for a *redo*. Nothing stops conflict in its tracks quicker than someone catching themselves and asking for that. Approach the conversation again from a better mindset and rephrase your complaint without attacking your partner's character or shortcomings.

And remember, even in the midst of a heated argument, there's still a deep yearning for connection.

If you or your partner use criticism to communicate dissatisfaction or frustration with each other, take it seriously. Your partner is your teammate. Come together and make this your number one relationship priority.

12.

Contempt:
Crossing the Line into Toxic Communication

What does contempt look like? And how do we tame that wild beast?

I remember the first time I recognized contempt in a couple. It was early in my coaching career. They would swing from language that was supportive and loving into nasty words and behaviors that showed utter contempt. When communication around sexual frequency broke down, leaving them stuck in a disagreement, expressions of contempt were their "go to" habit. It was clear that the intimacy they were seeking was never going to grow until they recognized the destructive nature of contempt.

Contempt is perhaps the most destructive of all relationship behaviors. When we treat our partners with contempt, we send a clear message that we don't value or respect them. This can have devastating effects on the health and longevity of a relationship.

Understanding the impact of contempt on couples

Contempt can take many forms, from name-calling and insults to sarcasm and eye-rolling. It often arises when we feel angry, frustrated, or disappointed with our partner. Instead of addressing the issue in a healthy and productive way, we allow our emotions to get the better of us, and we lash out.

The problem with contempt is that it creates a toxic cycle of negativity that can be very difficult to break. When we treat our partners with contempt, they're likely to respond with defensiveness, withdrawal, or stonewalling. This, in turn, can make us even more contemptuous, and the cycle continues.

The first example of contempt with my coaching couple was eye-rolling when one of them shared their thoughts or feelings about sexual frequency. The second expression of contempt was snide under the breath, comments when one of them was talking. This clearly communicated a lack of respect for the other person's feelings and opinions. This cycle eroded the emotional connection between them. They both felt lonely, resentful, and disconnected. Their relationship didn't offer them a place of retreat from the world. It had instead become a war zone that impacted their mental health. One of them struggled with ongoing anxiety, and the other was on constant high alert from the stress of conflict.

Recognizing and acknowledging contemptuous behavior

Let's look at the way contempt shows itself in a relationship:

Eye-rolling: When one partner rolls their eyes in response to something the other partner says, it communicates a lack of respect and a dismissive attitude.

Sarcasm: Sarcasm can come across as mocking or belittling, which can be hurtful to the partner on the receiving end and damaging to the emotional connection between.

Name-calling: When one partner uses derogatory names or insults in response to something the other partner says, it will erode the emotional connection between partners. Hurtful words linger for days, months, sometimes years.

Dismissive body language: When one partner crosses their arms, turns away, or makes other gestures that communicate a lack of interest or respect, it conveys a lack of empathy and understanding.

Criticism: Criticizing one's partner in a harsh or judgmental way creates resentment and hostility. While criticism is not the same thing as contempt, it can often be a precursor to contempt in a relationship.

Drawing a line in the sand

The couple I was coaching had become habituated to contempt because it fell within the familiar zone of their behavior patterns. It was time for them to draw a new line in the sand that they would not cross, no matter how heated emotions got. They started to recognize the destructive nature of contempt and made a commitment to treat each other with respect and kindness, even when they were angry. They had to step back and learn healthier ways to express their emotions, like using "I" statements and *active listening*. Most importantly, they stepped out of mutual blame and came together as a team in order to address the underlying issues. They made the very important decision to seek outside help to do that, and with that help, they began to feel safe enough with each other for intimacy to grow again.

Strategies for breaking the contempt habit

Breaking the habit of contempt can be challenging, but, with commitment and effort from both partners, it's possible. Here are some strategies that couples can use to break the cycle of contempt in their relationship:

Recognize and acknowledge the problem. The first step in addressing contempt is to acknowledge that it's a problem in the relationship. Both partners should be willing to take responsibility for their part in the dynamic and commit to working on the issue.

Practice active listening. Active listening is a technique where you listen to your partner's perspective without judgment or interruption. It's a powerful way to show empathy and understanding and break the cycle of contemptuous communication.

Replace negative behaviors with positive ones. Instead of rolling your eyes or making a sarcastic comment, try to show empathy for your partner's point of view (even if it's not your own). This can help to build a more positive and supportive dynamic in the relationship.

Practice gratitude. When making a request, develop the habit of expressing gratitude for the things that your partner does well or that you appreciate about them. Start with a gratitude statement followed by the request.This can help to shift the focus away from negative behaviors and build a more positive emotional connection.

Seek professional help. A therapist can help both partners identify the underlying issues that contribute to contemptuous behavior and provide tools and strategies for addressing the issue.

Breaking the habit of contempt can be challenging, but it's worth the effort. In a world so desperately in need of loving kindness, our contribution to a better world begins at home.

13.

Stonewalling:
Tearing Down the Walls, One Stone at a Time

Stonewalling is a form of emotional and physical withdrawal in which one relationship partner refuses to engage with the other partner in the midst of a conflict. If this is a pattern in a relationship, the wall of stone can become so high that neither partner can see over it. Stonewalling may involve a lack of response to a conversation, a refusal to discuss a point of conflict, or an unwillingness to find resolution. It can also be experienced as a physical withdrawal from a partner by walking away or avoiding being together in the same room (or in some cases the same bed).

Identifying patterns of behavior that lead to stonewalling

I'm inspired to talk about stonewalling because of discussions with one of my coaching couples. They both complained to me about a loss of emotional and physical intimacy in their relationship. They acknowledged that most of their intimacy challenges were based on resentment and unhealthy patterns of communication that generated bad feelings on a regular basis. I'll call them Eric and Shannon.

Eric grew up with family members who used anger as a way to control others. As a child, his response to that environment was to step away from the angry words and use stonewalling to punish the perpetrators and protect himself from feeling emotionally overwhelmed. But Eric's old stonewalling strategy was literally threatening his relationship. Stonewalling had become his most familiar way to bypass conflict with Shannon. In his mind, he was avoiding making things worse by removing himself from the threat and retreating emotionally.

To Shannon, Eric's stonewalling was the very behavior that created the most damage. In her mind it was often more damaging than the original conflict. She was hurt by Eric's disconnection from her. She felt ignored, rejected, and invalidated, and under her anger was sadness at the fear of losing Eric.

Eric was afraid to lose Shannon as well. While he had a head-in-the-sand approach to conflict, Shannon's strategy was to go head-to-head into battle by pushing through conflict and seeking resolution as soon as possible. Eric experienced this as confrontational and demanding. Her discomfort with a lack of immediate resolution would end up pushing Eric into *overwhelm*, which led him to stonewall Shannon (in order to keep her at bay). Every conflict would engage this pattern and send both of them into a mode of self-protection.

Creating healthy habits of communication

Eric and Shannon started to recognize their opposing strategies to avoid conflict and how they both contributed to triggering each other. They were able to avoid stonewalling before it happened by using their insights to develop new communication habits. One of those habits was understanding that they were both seeking the same thing — to be understood — and avoid the pain of conflict.

Eric learned to recognize the early signs of his emotional overwhelm. Now he calls for a time-out; not to punish Shannon but to take a much-needed break in order to calm down and process his feelings. He sees that his stonewalling only heightened Shannon's fears and insecurities, which made her push harder for a quick resolution. Now they both agree that before conflict ramps up into angry words, they will take a time-out. If Eric needs to leave the room to calm down (rather than stomping out, slamming doors, and stonewalling Shannon for a day or two) he reassures her that he'll be back in an agreed amount of time, whether it's five minutes, twenty minutes, or an hour. Eric's reassurance helps Shannon relax and trust that taking a time-out is not a form of punishment, but rather Eric's self-care. She sees that taking space helps both of them clear their minds, calm their nervous systems, and more effectively seek the resolution they both desire.

When a couple understands how their conflict strategies differ, they can begin to consider their needs, where those needs come from, and how to get them met. It's important to recognize that we are often different than our partner. Understanding our differences will help to bring an end to strategies like stonewalling.

14.

Defensiveness:
Breaking the Cycle in Your Relationship

Every one of Dr. John Gottman's Four Horsemen (Contempt, Stonewalling, Criticizing, Defensiveness) is a maladaptive strategy to protect us from harm. I'm sure you can trace your protective strategies back through the ages, even to the playground, when you were first introduced to these deadly relationship horsemen so many years ago.

"No, I'm not, you are!" "I didn't do it, you did!" "I didn't want to be your friend anyway!"

We learned very young how to deflect, defend, and deny in order to save us from perceived danger. It all made sense at the time, but now as adults in relationships, that same defensiveness shuts down constructive communication with a defensive word, or even just a look.

As adults in relationships, our defensiveness is just as transparent as it was in our younger years. Our vocabulary may have grown, but the strategy is still pretty simple: deflect and defend from attack.

"I'm not defensive, I'm just explaining myself." "Why are you attacking me? I'm not the one who started this." "I don't need to change. You're the one who needs to change." "It's not my fault. You started this."

These statements are defensive, they blame the other person, deny wrongdoing, or refuse to engage in a constructive dialogue. Instead of acknowledging our partner's perspective and seeking to find common ground, defensive statements escalate conflict and undermine emotional connection.

Strategies for Overcoming Defensiveness in Relationships

Fear of vulnerability is often at the root of defensiveness. Here are some factors that contribute to that fear:

Low self-esteem: People with low self-esteem may be more defensive because they are sensitive to criticism and feel threatened by it. They may fear that criticism or feedback will confirm their negative self-image, leading them to become defensive and protective of their self-esteem.

Insecurity: People who feel insecure in their relationships may be more defensive because they fear rejection or abandonment. They may perceive criticism or feedback as a threat to their connection with their partner, leading them to become defensive and protective of their relationship.

Trauma: People who have experienced trauma, abuse, or neglect may be more defensive because they have learned to protect themselves from harm. They may perceive criticism or feedback as a threat to their safety, leading them to become defensive and protective of themselves.

Communication style: Some people may have a communication style that is naturally more defensive, perhaps because they have learned to be assertive or to protect themselves from conflict or criticism.

Cultural factors: Cultural norms and values can also influence defensiveness. In some cultures, being defensive may be seen as a sign of strength or assertiveness, while in others, it may be seen as a weakness or a lack of humility.

There are many reasons that contribute to someone choosing defensiveness as their primary strategy, and they all feel equally bad.

Like all the Four Horsemen, defensiveness has a hardness to it. Just like the armor we imagine the horsemen wearing on their bodies, defensiveness looks and feels like a hardened shell of anger and protection.

The way through that hardness is to ask yourself: What am I protecting? What's the underlying fear behind the defense?

We can always choose to put our armor down and acknowledge that defensiveness is not going to make us any safer. In a relationship, safety comes only with connection, and connection comes only with vulnerability.

Dealing with the effects of defensiveness on a relationship

Here are some suggestions for the next time you find yourself armored up for defensive battle:

Be curious: Curiosity is the opposite of defense. Rather than becoming defensive, try to approach your partner's concerns with curiosity. Ask questions to understand their perspective. Instead of defaulting to reactivity, try being more responsive to what your partner is saying.

Cultivate empathy: Step into your frontal lobe which is your brain's seat of empathy. Empathy can help partners understand each other's perspectives and connect on a deeper level. By putting yourself in your partner's shoes, you can create a more supportive and understanding environment.

Take responsibility: Even if you don't agree with your partner's perspective, taking responsibility for your part in the situation or misunderstanding can defuse your defensiveness and help your partner feel heard.

Defensiveness can have damaging effects on a relationship with escalating conflict, communication breakdown, emotional distance, and the development of negative relationship patterns.

It is important for couples to recognize the signs of defensiveness and work together to address it in a constructive and positive way. If one of you uses defensiveness as your chosen armor, seek out the help you need to break the unhealthy patterns that are keeping you from living an undefended life.

15.

Finding the Gifts in Conflict: Diving Below the Surface Tension

No matter who you are or how happy you are in your relationship, you're going to experience conflict. Experiencing conflict in your relationship is not a sign of weakness, nor a lack of wisdom: It's simply a polarized dialogue between two people holding opposing positions. How we navigate this dialogue is determined by how skillful we are at moving through conflict as a couple.

The Saboteur mind versus the Sage mind

When it comes to our inner battles and moments of clarity, think of the "saboteur" as the nagging voice in your head, always pointing out flaws and holding you back. The saboteur is your personal critic. Meanwhile the "sage" is your inner guru, offering you wise advice and nudging you toward positive choices and self-awareness. This is the tussle we all suffer in our subjective experiences to one degree or another.

When our inner Saboteur is present in a conflict, emotions easily escalate. We create what is almost certainly a false story about our partner that's full of judgment and blame. Our Saboteur knows exactly what to say to make us right and our partner wrong. Sometimes we realize something we're about to say is damaging, but we say it anyway.

When our inner Sage is present in a conflict, we exercise our wisdom muscles and bring tools of understanding and curiosity to the conversation. *Our inner Sage listens more and reacts less.* It seeks reconciliation and steps back from the heat of the moment, to ask some important questions, like *why?*

Make an agreement with your partner that you'll ask each other *why* you've chosen your position in an argument — not in a demanding tone, but from a place of curiosity and a desire to understand. Once they've answered, ask them again, Why? And for a third time, ask them why. *Why* do they feel the way they do? *Why* is it important for them? Why?

Hearing the deeper "why" behind our positions is often missed in a heated argument. If we're in a triggered state, we jump over our underlying why's and make defense and survival our primary focus. We're operating from our primal brain in an effort to survive attack. We want to be proven right and convert our partner to our perspective.

Going deeper into our curiosity enough to ask "why" *three times* helps to intercept our Saboteur's fearful judgments and reveals the needs behind our partner's position. Asking why with the intention to really listen offers our partner a chance to reflect on their needs and the time to express themselves clearly. This process helps to awaken our empathy and step into our partner's shoes. Bypassing the pain of anger and finding resolution is a huge victory for a couple. Each victory builds the muscle memory of moving through disagreements quickly. The stronger those muscles become, the easier it is to find consensus and return to connection.

Rather than viewing conflict with a "grit your teeth and get through it" attitude, dig deeper and discover the gifts that can be found in conflict.

Gift #1 – Creating new patterns

With every conflict there's an opportunity to grow in and return to connection. We learn to recognize when our inner saboteurs are front and center, escalating emotions and armoring ourselves against the pain of disconnection. Choosing to de-escalate a conflict is the first and most difficult step to take, but this choice becomes easier with every success. With every de-escalation, we strengthen new and healthy patterns of managing conflict.

Gift #2 – Deepening trust

If you move through conflict led by your Sage mind, you will deepen trust and connection with your partner. You'll both begin to trust that conflict doesn't have to rattle your core or threaten your relationship. It doesn't have to pit one *right* person against one *wrong* person. Your Sage mind understands that conflict is a stepping- stone to effective communication, listening, and finding a new shared position that acknowledges the underlying needs of both people.

Gift #3 – Getting to what's true

Conflict offers us the opportunity to speak our truth. If we find disconnection scary, we will get into the habit of suppressing our needs. Withholding our truth as a way to avoid disconnection only leads to resentment and more conflict down the line. Having opposing positions with our partner offers us the opportunity to practice our communication skills. Intercept your Saboteur in its familiar mode of reactivity and accusations and embrace your Sage mind — which is curious about our partner's deeper "whys".

Healthy relationships allow conflicts to arise. Skilled couples have the tools to intercept their Saboteurs and adopt a Sage mind in order to create new patterns, deepen trust, and be heard in our truth. Consider a current or recent conflict you've had with your partner and imagine how you both might replace the angry voice of your Saboteur with the wisdom of your Sage. How would learning about your partner's more vulnerable underlying needs quiet the judgmental voice of your inner Saboteur? How would the conflict have progressed if each of your Sage minds took the time to ask "why" three times?

16.

It's Not You, It's Me:
Getting to the Core of Your Relationship
Saboteurs

Most couples who come to me for intimacy and relationship coaching have one thing in common: they want to know how to *get their partner to change*. They've become so used to paying attention to their partner's shortcomings that they've forgotten — or have chosen to ignore — their own 50 percent of the relationship equation. Getting to the core of our own relationship strategies and behavior patterns is crucial if a couple seeks lasting transformation. It not only improves their intimate relationship, but every relationship in their lives.

Our patterns of relating to others run deep. Most of us don't recognize how our patterns of behavior unconsciously run our lives and impact those around us. We want a better relationship, but rarely do we delve into the core strategies we've taken on in life to assess the role they play in our relationships with our partner. Chronic conflict, finger-pointing, complaining, judging, and blaming are all byproducts of unhealthy patterns and old programming. Before I work with a couple on their sensual life, I ask them to spend time doing some core relationship coaching with me. Understanding the patterns partners bring to their relationship is often the key that unlocks the door to deeper love, better sex, and authentic desire.

What do I mean by core relationship coaching?

We're all born into environments that challenge us, to a greater or lesser degree. As children, we quickly develop strategies to cope with those challenges (and even to survive). Even in the best families, no child escapes the experiences of fear, insecurity, sadness, and self-doubt. These challenges are built into our human development. Pull out an old photo of yourself under the age of 10 and take a good look into the eyes of that child. That child (you) had already developed coping strategies when this photo was taken. They'd formed belief systems about their self-worth, and they'd already begun to armor themselves from the pain that comes with being human.

In the beginning, our coping strategies appear to be our helpers. They protect us from life's slings and arrows. Later in life, these strategies might hinder us. Let's use bullying as an example. If we were bullied at home or on the playground, our helper may have shown up as

- introversion, to keep us alone and thus away from the threat of others;
- aggressiveness, to fight back, perhaps becoming bullies ourselves;
- pleasing, to ensure that others will like us and keep us safe;
- hyper-vigilance, by becoming suspicious and mistrustful of other's motives; and/or
- victimization, to feel validated in our feelings of betrayal and gain the attention or sympathy we feel we deserve.

Our innate ability to survive as children was tailored to our environment and sometimes modeled by those closest to us. By observing our parents, our siblings, and our community, we learned ways to cope with the challenges life threw at us. The fact that we grew into adults proves our helpers did their job. However...

Q: When do our adaptive childhood helpers turn into our maladaptive adult saboteurs?

A: When the same strategies that helped us cope as children create obstruction to intimacy and connection in our adult relationships.

What literally felt life-threatening when we were eight years old no longer poses the same threat to us as adults. We may have successfully protected ourselves from the pain of bullying, but we've consciously or unconsciously decided to keep those helpers around. Our childhood protector is no longer our ally. It's now one of our saboteurs that feeds us with beliefs that no longer serve our happiness.

Even though we no longer experience bullying on the playground, our strategy of being introverted, aggressive, pleasing, suspicious, or victimized has become an ingrained part of how we operate in relationships today. What was once adaptive and helpful in protecting us at eight years of age has become maladaptive and harmful in our adult relationships. Until we recognize the nature of our maladaptive strategies and how they sabotage our relationships, we're locked into unconscious programming and reactivity that can cause a lifetime of conflict and disconnection. If you've ever seen a profile photo of an iceberg, your maladaptive programming is the large mass of ice under the surface. It's huge and, as we know, not visible from the surface.

This is what relationship coaching uncovers. It reveals what's under the surface and gives us powerful tools to clear our life of old programming that no longer serves us. It helps support self-awareness and self-compassion by acknowledging the usefulness old helpers once offered, and it welcomes in new programming and belief systems that support harmony in our adult relationships.

Brain training as a couple

Relationship coaching shows us we're always able to choose our thoughts. It's just that most of us are so adept at choosing the negative thoughts, we may have forgotten we have a choice in the matter! Insights empower us, but it's what we do with them that generates actual, tangible differences in our day-to-day life with our partner. That's why my couples incorporate brief daily practices that rewire neural pathways in the brain. Just like going to the gym to increase our physical strength, we build emotional strength and capacity to create new neural pathways, replacing old limiting patterns with the wisdom that comes from awareness and practice.

Relationship coaching is like looking at your relationship through a brand-new lens. When conflict arises my coaching couples approach it as an opportunity to use their new tools. They draw on a common language to understand themselves and each other better, and they realize (often for the first time) that happy relationships aren't mysterious accidents that only happen for the lucky ones.

17.

The Curse of Confirmation Bias: How We Look for Proof to Support Our Negative Stories

Confirmation bias: We all have it. We experience it every day in the news, our politics, our workplace, and (most directly) in our relationships, where partners can suffer the consequences daily. Humans are wired to look for danger, and danger in relationships comes in the form of complaints and conflict. Conflict triggers threat, and threat pumps cortisol into our bloodstream, preparing us for "fight or flight." So when it comes to relationships, it makes sense that our brains are far more skilled at noticing what's *wrong* with our partner than what's *right*.

We all form biases in order to make sense of our experiences. Those biases then form the basis of the stories we tell ourselves when we feel challenged by our partner. We look for the proof that supports the stories we already have written in our minds. If circumstances leave enough room for us to skew our interpretation of events, we'll jump on the opportunity to be right, even if it makes us feel bad.

An older couple I've counseled for some time is trying to heal from infidelity on the woman's part. Even though the infidelity happened years ago, her partner's negative feelings about the matter remain firmly in place. The story he formed from his bias is that she doesn't love him, that he's not a good lover, and that — given the opportunity — she'll betray his trust again (even though she repeatedly reassures him that none of those things are true).

The situation is corrosive to their relationship. If she has to work late, he imagines the worst. If she doesn't want to have sex one night, he creates the story that she finds sex with him boring. If she doesn't stop what she's doing immediately when he needs attention, he tells himself that she no longer loves him. You can see how his negative and fearful beliefs are his own worst enemy and may very well lead to a self-fulfilling prophecy.

When our relationships are laden with negative biases, we're on the constant lookout for proof that we're right, and we selectively overlook all the information that proves otherwise. We'll place great importance on the disappointing moments and pay less attention to the positive ones. By focusing on the negative encounters with your partner, you'll live your relationship assuming the worst, and you'll probably get what you're looking for. In other words, whatever you put your attention on will become your destiny.

You can actually *change your mind*. Start to steer your brain toward the positives by introducing some simple habits into your daily life. This is how we rewire our brains, and it's scientifically proven to help change the lens through which we interpret our world. Let's consider some solutions:

Give positive feedback to your partner about the things they did that day: You can do this in two ways: Actively look for the things your partner does that you appreciate and express your appreciation out loud regularly throughout the day. Form a gratitude practice with your partner. At night before you go to sleep, take turns expressing three things you appreciated about each other that day.

"I appreciated you asking me what I needed in town before you came home."

"I appreciated the way you handled the issue with the neighbors."

"I appreciated you pulling me close to cuddle tonight while watching TV."

When we point out what makes us feel cared for and loved, we're not only training our brains to notice the positives, but we're also training our partners by affirming their positive actions. (Yes, just like dog training!)

Become a positive Jedi: Get good at shifting from negative to positive. Think of this skill like a Jedi warrior. When you find yourself sinking into the dark world of complaint and disappointment, remind yourself that there's a lighter, brighter world that's just as (or even more) true. Look for the positives with Jedi-like precision. As you work on this skill you'll build the muscle of your positive intelligence, making it easier to shift from negative to positive with ease.

Seek resolution rather than sweeping conflict under the rug: We're particularly susceptible to selective memory if conflicts with our partner are left unresolved. Lack of resolution keeps a negative incident active in our brains. Once an argument feels resolved, our brain files the event away as a memory, relieving us of ongoing rumination and the biases that are formed by keeping that negative event in the forefront of our memory.

Learn communication skills that lead you through conflict to resolution. This is the primary marker of a long-lasting happy relationship. Since we're the only ones in charge of creating our stories and forming our negative biases, why not consider adopting a positive bias? Assume the best of your partner. With every single complaint, look for five expressions of appreciation. And note how this impacts your daily exchanges as well as your mental state.

18.

Addicted to Love:
Hormonal Cocktails That Keep Us
Coming Back For More

> *Your lights are on, but you're not home*
> *Your mind is not your own*
> *Your heart sweats, your body shakes*
> *Another kiss is what it takes*
>
> *You can't sleep, you can't eat*
> *There's no doubt, you're in deep*
> *Your throat is tight, you can't breathe*
> *Another kiss is all you need*
>
> — Robert Palmer, *You're Addicted to Love*

Ask most couples about the early stages of their relationship, and they'll remember the ease they experienced around sex and intimacy. They'll stare off into space with memories of testosterone-driven lust and estrogen-flooded seduction. They may remember how the initial feelings of lust began to grow into romantic longing and preoccupation as their bodies started producing more dopamine and norepinephrine.

At some point — usually between three and fifteen months — the intoxication of new relationship energy (NRE) begins to shift from high levels of passion to attachment. Oxytocin, the love hormone, then starts to lay the foundation for the security of long-term partnership. Understanding the biology of sex and intimacy helps explain why couples often ask, "How do we get the passion back into our sex lives? Why don't we feel the way we used to?"

That's nature for you!

We're made to reproduce, and our bodies know exactly what hormones support that undeniable human drive. If you want to re-ignite that NRE, take charge and stimulate the hormones that got you there in the first place. Here are the building blocks that will produce a cocktail of hormones to support deep connection and a vibrant sex life:

Attachment

Oxytocin fuels our desire to bond with our partners. It creates the romance of "you and me against the world." Love notes, kisses in the kitchen, long hugs, hand-holding, and cuddling lead to trust and goodwill between partners. Oxytocin sets the stage for expressions of love that make partners receptive and vulnerable with each other. Feelings of attachment get us through the rough spots. Oxytocin keeps us steady and invested in each other's happiness.

Communication

Dedicate some of your time together to manufacturing some serotonin. You do this by getting vulnerable and sharing your feelings with one another. Step out of the day-to-day chit-chat about the details of living and dig a little deeper. Don't be afraid to talk to your partner about your relationship. Ask them to share what ways you can be a better partner to them. Caring and being cared for reinforces your bond and your sense that your partner has your back. This experience of secure attachment in a relationship brings a sense of harmony to every other part of life. If your partner can count on you supplying them with a hit of serotonin whenever you're together, that will stimulate their reward centers. Give them some heartfelt communication on a regular basis and watch what happens.

Novelty

You can create dopamine in your body by doing new things together; sharing new experiences, new places, trips, and (yes) *hotel rooms*. When I ask a couple to recall a hot sexual memory they have together, it will often involve a hotel room. They stepped out of the familiar bedroom, family routine, daily tasks – basically a life you can walk through with your eyes closed because you know it so well. Suddenly the desire they'd been missing started flowing again. They started to see their partner through the eyes of the goddess dopamine.

Sex in a long-term partnership can easily become predictable. You don't have to become someone new to add variety to your together time, although some role-play can be fun. I've outlined 186 erotic activities from sensual to kinky in my e-book *Your Erotic Menu*. If you want more variety in your sexual and sensual life, look there to see all the options you and your partner can explore. *Your Erotic Menu* online course is my gift to you. You'll find your exclusive access link to the course in Your Next Steps at the end of this book.

Adventure

Our bodies produce an interesting cocktail of hormones when we challenge ourselves physically. Adrenaline, endorphins, and testosterone all get a boost from any type of physical adventure or challenge. Aerobic workouts, dancing, hiking, biking, and other exercise have all been shown to increase circulation, blood flow, and lubrication — three factors involved in heightened sexual desire. Set an adventure date with your partner. Hit the road or paddle the white waters. Use your bodies together and experience the aphrodisiac effects of endorphins.

Mystery

Couples are often under the impression that there's nothing they don't know about their partner. We've all heard the expression "familiarity breeds contempt." While we may not be feeling contempt for our partner, we can take our partner for granted and end up assuming we know everything there is to know. Seeing our partners as individuals outside of the relationship creates dopamine, which is associated with a sense of mystery.

When our bodies produce dopamine, our partner seems new and exciting. We become intrigued again and refreshed in our view of this person with whom we share a bed every night. In order to maintain mystery in a long-term relationship, you want an ongoing balance of attachment and independence. Too much of either will tilt the scale away from desire. Too much distance, and we lose our sense of bonding. Never spending time apart from each other will send you into the roommate zone. Find ways of taking space and doing your own thing. See friends, exercise, or start a new sport or hobby that engages you. Differentiate yourself from your partner in healthy ways. Romantic attachment is important to build trust and safety, but creating space from your partner is the necessary ingredient to building desire.

The tide can't come flooding back to the shore if it never goes out in the first place. Catch my drift?

19.

I Beg Your Pardon?
Who's the Bully in Your Relationship?

I woke up one morning feeling emotionally battered by some news footage I'd watched the night before that included bullying behavior by a politician. I thought about people who currently live (or have lived) with an adult bully. I wondered how many of them were left triggered by the painful display of the bully strategy on TV.

Bullying can happen in every form of relationship from the bedroom to the boardroom. I see subtle and not-so-subtle forms of bullying with many of my coaching couples. I've boiled it down to nine ways to recognize that there's a bully in your intimate relationship.

But first consider that if you were able to ask someone during a bullying incident to be transparently honest about what's driving their bullying, they'd probably identify *fear* as their underlying emotion, *insecurity* as their underlying feeling, and *control* as their underlying strategy. They're using bullying to fend off painful feelings of inferiority and disrespect.

Many adult bullies come from childhood homes where these very fears reflected their reality, and where they too were dominated by emotional bullying. Those who have their sense of control taken from them will commonly seek to control others, often with the same tactics they witnessed in the adults around them. What's harder to acknowledge though, is our *own* inner bully — the part of us that jumps into action when we're backed into a corner and feel trapped. We're all capable of resorting to bullying tactics in our relationship, should our partner challenge our beliefs and perspectives.

Most of us would never call ourselves bullies. We'd rather see ourselves as passionate, intense, direct, strong-willed, or generally superior in our perspective of what's right or wrong. We may even admit that we're too much for some people, but "that's just who I am." Yet the fact is, we're all capable of reverting back to the playground when we're triggered into fight or flight. When anger floods your brain, even the most self-aware person can turn to bullying tactics. You're literally not in your right mind; you're in your amygdala brain, which is pumping adrenaline into your bloodstream. It's focused on survival or (in the case of an argument) on being proven right.

Let's look at the behavior of an emotional bully in an intimate relationship. I think you'll see that we all have an inner bully that can hijack a conversation and turn it into emotional manipulation in order to get something we want.

Getting angry and raising your voice takes the focus off the disagreement and places it on the management of your emotional state. Your partner will want to settle you down. They'll either join you in the ramp-up that leads to painful words and hurt feelings, or they'll appease you and stifle themselves to keep the peace.

Blaming and pointing the finger back at your partner may have worked as a child but it's a sadly transparent attempt to avoid taking responsibility or hearing a difficult truth. Our inner bully has very little capacity for honest self-reflection and vulnerability. Criticism is equal to a personal attack and the defense of a bully is to quickly divert the same criticism back to their partner. "I didn't lie, you're the liar!"

Punishing by emotionally pulling away, implementing the silent treatment, withholding affection, sulking, and moping, are all common strategies to punish our partner. These are the kind of bullying tactics to which a passive-aggressive person will resort in order to get their way. If your partner knows there's a price to pay for disagreeing with you, they'll likely choose to let you have your way and once again suppress their truth in exchange for an apparently peaceful home.

Threatening to leave the relationship is a common bullying strategy that gets tossed into the ring of a disagreement. It takes the conflict from a difference of opinion and amps it up to a potentially relationship-destroying prospect.

Gaslighting is a term the psychiatric community uses to describe when a partner slowly tries to confuse and manipulate perceptions. We can say one thing and do another. We can turn our partner's questions back on them, causing them to doubt themselves. We deny something in the face of proof. We're all susceptible to gaslighting and we're all fully capable of resorting to gaslighting. Remember, your inner bully is well-versed in getting what they want.

Name-calling takes a disagreement to a personal level. This is where lines are crossed, and painful words cut deep. Once you revert to name-calling, the damage is sometimes impossible to undo. The bond is broken, and trust is lost. Your partner may find their way back to being civil and even loving, but in their heart, the names you called them will resonate and resurface, sometimes for years.

Out-arguing your partner is the bully's way of pushing their opponents into the ropes and pummeling them with jabs to the ribs.

You wear them out with the words coming out of your mouth. Even when they've conceded you make sure to drive it home until they either go silent, beg you to stop, or leave the room.

Interrupting your partner when they're trying to make their point is another way a bully can wear someone down. When we don't have the capacity to listen to an opposing view without talking over our partner, we're shutting them down. This is a common form of bullying in relationships, and often both partners will adopt this strategy to be heard when conflicts start to escalate.

Physical intimidation is more than waving your fist at your partner. It's how you physically position yourself next to them. It's leaning in too close. It's looming over them. It's throwing a plate or slamming a door. It's driving erratically or blocking an exit. These are all acts of violence, and bullies use them as coercion and intimidation tactics.

Allowing your inner bully to represent you in an argument with your partner is short-sighted. It's looking for the short-term gain of being *proven right* over the long-term desire of *maintaining connection*. Your inner bully views your partner as the enemy to be conquered and controlled in a moment of conflict, rather than your teammate who shares your life with you.

Sit down together and review these signs of bullying. I strongly believe we're all guilty of these tactics in our worst moments, so go easy on yourself. Get hip to what bullying looks like in your relationship, and agree to being called out, when you let your inner bully take to the stage of a debate. Share the fears that drive your inner bully. Reflect on the family dynamic that made bullying part of your strategy to get what you want. And if you have children, tell them that what they see in our politicians these days does not represent healthy adult behavior!

20.

Infidelity:
Ten Steps to Unpacking the Pain

> *"I used to think I knew who I was, who he was, and suddenly I don't recognize us, neither him nor me... My entire life, as I've led it up to this moment, has crumbled, like in those earthquakes where the very ground devours itself and vanishes beneath your feet while you're making your escape. There is no turning back."*
>
> — Simone de Beauvoir, *The Woman Destroyed*

I had a question from a client about infidelity. They wanted to know how best to heal their relationship with their partner. The feelings of betrayal that come from an affair being discovered can be overwhelming. Our world that felt safe one minute now feels dangerous and threatening. We can't think straight, adrenaline courses through our bodies, and we shift from a calm, logical mind into fight, flight, or freeze. When we feel triggered or threatened, our amygdala brain runs the show. Its sole purpose is to protect us from perceived threats and keep us alive.

For a couple going through infidelity and betrayal, this little bit of brain science is extremely important to understand. Every living being is constantly scanning to avoid danger and find safety, so it's not surprising that we're also on alert for danger in our relationships. Every day of our lives we're assessing. Are we safe in our mother's arms? Are we safe with our new best friend? Are we safe with the person we sleep beside every night?

When we choose a partner to settle down with, it's because we've found some sense of safety with them. It takes time and emotional investment to establish trust and safety. We all know that panicky transition point in a new relationship where we realize we've become attached. We have some skin in the game and are vulnerable to being emotionally hurt. This is why early stages of a relationship can feel like a rollercoaster, until we find the feeling of safety our brain seeks. As the relationship progresses, our insecurities begin to fade. Trust is built over time, based on consistency and demonstration.

Once we've established feelings of safety with our partner, and trust that we're not at risk of emotional pain, we can relax and settle. We commit to each other, promising to have each other's backs. We agree to attach more deeply and join as a team. This feeling of safety, that every couple works so hard to create, takes a hit when it comes to infidelity. If you suddenly don't feel safe in your relationship, getting back to safety is your first phase of healing.

Here are 10 steps to start rebuilding trust and safety after infidelity:

1. It's okay to not know

You may both be confused right now. You may not know whether to stay together or not. Write this down on a note and stick it on your mirror: "It's okay to not know." Time will bring clarity. You're in the middle of a process right now. Allow clarity to emerge. Don't force each other to be further along than you are. When you're not feeling safe, it's a good time to take care of your nervous system and postpone life-changing decisions.

2. Less you, more them

If you're the one who broke a monogamous agreement, you may be feeling immense guilt and shame. Don't make it all about you. Don't get stuck in self-defense. Stay focused on your partner's needs right now. Express regret: say how sorry you are, but stay empathetic to their feelings. Stay steady and help them feel heard and accepted in all their emotions.

3. The "why"

You may be spending a lot of time initially talking about who, where, and when, but also get curious about *why*. What was the motivating desire behind the affair? What unmet needs caused one of you to look outside the relationship? Needs for desire and affection, novelty, validation, sexual excitement, are just a few reasons that lead us into another's arms. Reasons for an affair might be based on what we're not getting from our partner, or they may be based on what we're not finding within ourselves. Transgressors can discover a part of themselves they've lost along the way. Examining the reasons for an affair is key to moving forward.

4. Talk less, listen more

Learn to communicate effectively. Slow down. Ask questions to learn more about your partner's perspective. If you find yourself getting triggered, ask for a time-out so you can regroup, breathe deeply, and return in a calmer state. If you were a team before the infidelity, you can be a team after as well.

5. The need behind the emotion

Understand that being triggered or lashing out is a response to not feeling safe. If your partner is swimming in negative emotions, help them by asking what they need from you to feel safe and then give it to them. This is not a time for your explanations or self-defense. Ask them what you can do to calm their inner storm. Hold or cradle them. Listen to them express what they're feeling without trying to fix them. These are ways to help each other calm down and begin the journey back to trust and safety. Even if your future feels unclear in the moment, you can access empathy and compassion to ease the pain.

6. The tango rule

At some point, ideally with the help of a professional, both partners need to explore how their behaviors may have contributed to the affair. Without placing all the blame on the betrayer or dwelling in self-condemnation on the part of the betrayed, both partners need to engage in a two-way examination. This can sometimes be tricky for a partner who chooses to only view themselves as a victim. What I've found is that when partners are willing to dig deep and be honest, there are sides to the story of infidelity to which both people can speak. Taking the role of victim out of the equation helps create a path to accountability and self-awareness.

7. Strong and sturdy baby steps

Build trust and safety slowly. If you're the transgressor, you'll want to ensure you keep the small agreements you make with your partner. Be on time, do what you say you'll do, be generous with your attention, initiate moments of intimate sharing, and inquire about your partner's needs when you sense they're feeling unsafe or triggered. Small things can be blown out of proportion because resentment, hurt, or anger are still running the show, so be aware of the undercurrents and try to meet the needs behind the emotions. Your partner's amygdala is not going to have a rational conversation with you. Focus on reestablishing safety for your partner first.

8. Don't sweep things under the rug

This is not a problem the transgressor can skirt around by avoiding the topic and denying the complex emotions your partner is experiencing (even if they too are bypassers). You must go through it together to get to the other side. It's easy to want to bypass something that makes us feel bad about ourselves, but your partner needs you to be the anchor in their storm of emotions. If you sense your partner is in the pain of rumination or feeling insecure, don't wait for them to have to speak about it. Don't let them suffer silently in their thoughts. Tell them what they need to hear in that moment to reassure them. Stay afloat and learn to guide them back to calm waters without drowning in your own pain of shame and regret.

9. Build back better

Acknowledge that the infidelity may mean the end of your relationship *as it was.* You now have the opportunity to build a new relationship with your partner — one based on honesty and vulnerability. Revisit your mutual agreements and expectations around monogamy. Learn about the power of forgiveness and why it's important for both of you. Relationship problems push us outside of our comfort zone and force us to expand and mature. I've seen couples come out of infidelity closer than ever, humbled in their humanness, and able to repair and move forward.

10. Gratitude x 3

Each night before sleep, practice gratitude with each other. Find even the smallest things and start there. Choose three things each and say them out loud while you're lying in bed together. Remind your partner every day that you have gratitude for what they bring to your life, what they did that day that you appreciated, and what you love about them. Use this practice to reframe challenging emotions and fall asleep with a grateful heart.

These 10 steps are phase one of your healing process. Don't feel you have to go down this road alone. It can be dark and treacherous without someone shining the light for you. Infidelity is just one part of your relationship journey. It doesn't have to be the end of the road. Your relationship can survive infidelity, but it can't survive divorce.

21.

Loving Your Inner Child: A Work in Progress

> *Our partners do not belong to us; they are only on loan, with an option to renew — or not. Knowing that we can lose them does not have to undermine commitment; rather, it mandates an active engagement that long-term couples often lose. The realization that our loved ones are forever elusive should jolt us out of complacency in the most positive sense.*
>
> — Esther Perel, *The State of Affairs*

We are walking, talking, memory machines. We draw information from old memories and apply it to our present-day decisions. Every pleasure to which we're drawn, every pain we avoid, every relationship dynamic or conflict pulls from these memories to guide our physical and emotional experiences in the present moment.

Interestingly, the memories that most impact our adult emotional state took place long ago, when challenging childhood experiences began to form our strategies for surviving in a dangerous world. Challenging childhood experiences shape our beliefs, behaviors, and emotional responses as well as how we perceive and interact with the world around us.

Here are some examples:

Emotional Regulation: Challenging childhood experiences can impact our ability to regulate our emotions, leading to difficulties managing stress, anxiety, or depression.

Self-Esteem: Our childhood experiences impact our self-esteem and sense of worth, which can impact our confidence and ability to pursue our goals in adulthood.

Cognitive Patterns: Negative childhood experiences can shape our thought patterns and lead to negative self-talk, limiting beliefs, and cognitive distortions that impact our mental health and overall well-being.

Coping Strategies: Challenging childhood experiences can impact the coping strategies we use to manage stress or emotional pain. Unhealthy coping strategies, such as substance abuse or self-harm, can have lasting impacts on our lives.

Exploring attachment styles

Attachment styles in relationships refer to patterns of behavior and beliefs about intimacy and closeness that individuals develop based on their early experiences with caregivers. There are four main attachment styles: secure, anxious-preoccupied, dismissive-avoidant, and fearful-avoidant.

Secure Attachment: Individuals with a secure attachment style feel comfortable with intimacy and are able to trust their partners. They have positive views of themselves and their relationships, and they are generally able to communicate openly and resolve conflicts effectively. They feel secure in their relationships and can balance independence with closeness.

Examples:

"I feel comfortable expressing my needs and emotions to you, and I trust that you'll be there for me when I need support."

"Even when we have disagreements, I know that we can work through them together and come out stronger on the other side."

"I feel secure when we're apart, knowing that you love me and have my back."

Anxious-Preoccupied Attachment: Individuals with an anxious-preoccupied attachment style often crave closeness and fear rejection from their partners. They may be overly sensitive to relationship dynamics, constantly seeking reassurance and validation. They may struggle with self-doubt and have difficulty trusting their partners, leading to a pattern of clinginess and dependence.

Examples:

"Do you still love me? I need constant reassurance that you won't leave me, and I worry that you'll find someone better."

"I can't stop thinking about us and whether we're okay. Why haven't you texted me back yet? Did I do something wrong?"

"I feel like I'm always the one reaching out and trying to keep our relationship going. Am I just not enough for you?"

Dismissive-Avoidant Attachment: Individuals with a dismissive-avoidant attachment style tend to value independence and self-reliance over emotional intimacy. They may avoid closeness and vulnerability in relationships, preferring to maintain a sense of autonomy. They may downplay the importance of emotional connection and may struggle to express their feelings or needs to their partners.

Examples:

"I don't need anyone else to make me happy. I'm fine on my own, and I don't want to feel tied down by anyone."

"Why do you always want to talk about your feelings? Can't we just enjoy each other's company without all this emotional stuff?"

"I need my space right now. Can't you see that I need time to myself? I don't want to feel smothered by your constant need for closeness."

Fearful-Avoidant Attachment: Individuals with a fearful-avoidant attachment style experience a combination of anxiety and avoidance in relationships. They desire closeness but are also fearful of intimacy and potential rejection. They may oscillate between seeking connection and withdrawing from their partners, struggling to find a balance between their need for closeness and their fear of getting hurt.

Examples:

"I want to be close to you, but I'm afraid of getting hurt again. It's easier for me to push you away than to risk getting hurt."

"I'm torn between wanting to be with you and wanting to protect myself from getting hurt. I don't know how to navigate this push-pull dynamic."

"I feel like I'm always on edge in our relationship, never knowing if you'll stay or leave. I want to trust you, but I'm afraid of getting my heart broken."

Of course, these examples are simplified, and attachment styles can be more complex and nuanced. Attachment styles aren't written in stone. Our inner child beliefs can change and grow based on new healing experiences and self-awareness. When my clients are triggered, and feeling emotionally challenged, I encourage them to ask themselves, how would you speak to a child? What words would you use to calm them, reassure them, and support them? Now, use those same words to speak to your inner child. Give your inner child the secure love they may have been missing so long ago. We can change the painful past by offering ourselves loving-kindness and support in the present.

Comforting your inner child

Comforting your inner child is a powerful way to address old wounds and heal from the past. Here are some steps for comforting your inner child when you feel triggered:

Identify the Trigger: The first step is to identify what's triggering you in the present moment. This could be a situation, behavior, or comment from your partner that reminds you of a past trauma or emotional wound. If you find your emotions are bigger than you'd expect, you can trust that the pain is coming from an old wound.

Acknowledge Your Inner Child: Once you've identified the trigger, take a moment to acknowledge the emotions and needs of your inner child. This means recognizing that your current emotional response is a result of unhealed wounds from your past.

Practice Self-Compassion: Offer yourself compassion and kindness in the moment. Remind yourself that it's okay to feel triggered and that your emotions are valid. This can help you feel more grounded and present.

Use Self-Soothing Techniques: Find ways to soothe yourself in the moment. This could be via deep breathing, visualization, or other mindfulness practices. You might also try journaling or talking to a trusted friend or therapist.

Reconnect with Your Inner Child: Finally, take time to connect with your inner child and offer comfort and reassurance. Imagine yourself as a child and offer words of love and support. You might also visualize your adult self holding and comforting your inner child.

Caring for your inner child takes practice and patience. If we hold judgment or blame toward our inner child, it can be hard to face our own lack of self-love and self-worth as adults; yet inner child work can be a powerful way to improve our present-day relationship challenges, with ourselves and our partner. Ultimately, the decision to engage in inner child work is a personal one. It's important to approach this work with an open mind and heart, and to be gentle with yourself as you explore your past experiences and emotions.

As a hypnotherapist, I have seen the power of suggestion turn a past negative outcome into one that is healed and resolved. Our early experiences do not have to define the rest of our lives and relationships. It's possible to heal from past trauma and difficulty.

22.

Empathy:
An Act of Generosity

NOTE: *This chapter was written at the height of the COVID lockdowns and remains useful and relevant for couples living in close proximity or with other forms of stress.*

We can all agree we're on a wild ride, worldwide! With the combination of less distractions and long-term confinement, storms of emotions may arise. I'd like to offer couples three steps to help navigate those troubled waters.

The next time your partner is letting loose and expressing their fear of uncertainty (or frustration with family dynamics, work-related anxiety, existential angst, grief of loss, overwhelm from the "new normal," or any other challenging emotion) say these words to yourself:

"I don't have to try to fix this right now."

Then take a breath and plant your feet in place like a massive tree in the forest. Tell yourself you're going to hold the space for your partner's emotional storm to pass without reacting, defending, accusing or all the other egoic traps we fall into for fear of *feeling wrong*. Your job — or rather your *opportunity* — is to meet the moment with emotional generosity.

I've coached men in doing this for their women, but it works both ways. No one is immune to overwhelm, and we can take turns showing up for each other in ways that make space for emotions that need to come out. If you're a "fixer" (and most of us are) and your partner starts to unleash their emotions, you probably feel immediate stress in your body. Your mind starts to race toward possible solutions before they've even finished speaking. You're no longer really listening while your brain scans for something to say, suggest, or act upon. You want to fix their problem because you love them and because you want the storm to stop.

But here's the thing: While you're racking your brain with strategies and solutions to calm them down, you're bypassing what they need the most right then and there. So, after you remind yourself that *you don't have to fix their problem*, step out of fix-it mode and turn toward them with your *whole body*. Listen to the words coming out of their mouth. Make eye contact and show them they have your *loving attention*.

This is where you become the tree that withstands the storm. You ground yourself deep into the earth and bring that strong presence to your partner. In that moment they need nothing more than to speak those words to someone who's letting them do just that. They need to express themselves, to move that energy out of their body, to feel what they're feeling and be witnessed in it.

Next, show empathy for what they're feeling. This doesn't mean you have to agree with their perspective if it's not yours. You're empathizing with their *feelings*, not the *content* of their story. Showing empathy simply acknowledges that your partner is feeling something difficult. When we empathize with another, we attune to their experience and feelings. We're looking inside of ourselves and connecting to that same feeling. Empathy is an active and intentional response to another person's feelings.

Teresa Wiseman, a nurse scholar who studies empathy, explains it like this:

"Empathy is perspective taking. It's the ability to take the perspective of another person. It's recognizing feelings in other people and then communicating that recognition back to them."

These are great skills to bring to any relationship when emotional storms arise. Imagine what it's like to be them in that moment. Put yourself in their place, and now respond from there. You might say something like,

"I'm sorry you're having a hard time. That must be difficult for you. Tell me more about that."

And mean it! Listen until they feel like they've said everything. If you feel more questions will help, use questions to guide them away from details and toward their feelings. "How are you feeling right now?" you might ask. These are the questions that will help them release negative emotions. If you're truly listening with an interest in how they're feeling, they'll feel heard. And in the end, no matter what the problem is, we all want to feel like someone hears us and cares.

You'll know when your partner feels heard. Their body will tell you! They'll start to slow down, their nervous system will calm, and they'll begin to breathe more deeply. Once they feel heard, they'll start to drop down into the deeper, more vulnerable feelings that underlie the overwhelm. This is what you want to support. Show them that they can lean on you (literally).

At this point you can offer some physical comfort. Let them feel that you've got them. Touch their arm. Hold them. Cradle them. Massage their feet or shoulders. Touch calms and nurtures us. In fact, sometimes touch is all we need to begin to let go and relax.

Once you've helped them back to a calmer, more centered place, maybe it's time to help them consider solutions to their problem (if they're solvable). But unless you master the skills of helping your partner feel *heard* in their emotional storms first, looking to fix something is not going to help in the moment. This is emotional generosity.

When we stop what we're doing and turn toward our partner, attune to their experience, and offer touch as a way to comfort and nurture, we find our deep well of emotional generosity.

23.

Ritual:
Infusing the Mundane with Meaning

On a trip to the snowy woods of Northern Wisconsin, I curled up in front of a fire to read a book on Japanese folk religions — a fitting subject for a natural environment that evokes stillness and silence in a busy mind. The Japanese culture is synonymous with ritual — particularly ritual tied to nature's rhythm and beauty. Shrines, festivals, purification rites, ceremonies, and ancestral veneration all bring meaning to Japanese life and culture. The interest in ritual (consider the Japanese tea ceremony) likely evolved as a coping mechanism for a dense population compacted onto a small island.

Rituals invite us to go deeper: deeper into the meaning behind our actions. They speak to a part of us that honors the *power of intention*.

What "rituals" exist in your life and relationship right now? Is there a ritual that, given more conscious intention, could deepen your connection with love and life?

Our lives are filled with rituals we inherited from our upbringing, as well as rituals we create that are unique to our own lives. Even the most mundane daily activities — like sharing a morning coffee or lighting a candle at dinner — can be elevated into a ritual by empowering the purpose of that activity.

A common ritual is putting aside quality time to be intimate, both physically and emotionally. "Quality time" can last a weekend, an evening, an hour or even a moment. If partners acknowledge the intention of being together, they can turn a simple hug into a ritual. If a couple agrees that the purpose of an extended hug is to drop into a connected space of appreciation and love, then a hugging ritual is born! If serving a cup of tea to your partner is done with the full intention to offer that cup with all your love, in service, then you have brought ritual to that ordinary daily gesture. If opening the car door for your partner is a ritual, you accept that service as a reminder to show your appreciation, and you do it with full attention and a smile. By visiting a beautiful vista that has meaning to you as a couple, you can share the intention of renewing your connection. When we agree to express three things for which we're grateful before we go to sleep at night, we bring a ritual of positivity and fullness into our slumber.

What moments in your relationship deserve to be ritualized and honored? I encourage couples to explore rituals in the bedroom. By preparing the room for intimacy by using lighting, music, scent, and fabric, we transform our intimate preparation into ritual. By showering or bathing, shaving, and performing other hygienic activities, we create the ritual of offering our bodies to our beloved and receiving their body in return.

Here's a suggestion: When you enter that prepared intimate space, light a candle together, and speak your intention for that time together:

> "My intention is to be here with you completely, and let go of all the mental chatter in my head."

"My intention is to feel my love and appreciation for having some time alone with you."

"My intention is to let go and receive pleasure."

When we can identify and speak our intention, it empowers us to make it so. When we hear our partner's intention, we can support them in making it so.

Rituals have been an integral part of human life throughout history. These days many people have moved away from traditional rituals or forgotten the importance of creating new ones. In order to reengage rituals into our lives, we can start by having a conversation with our partner and making a conscious effort to incorporate them into our daily routines.

24.

Nonviolent Communication: Eight Tips to Move Through Conflict

If you're in a relationship with another human, disagreements will happen. It's a given. No matter how much you love someone, you can't avoid holding differing opinions and engaging in heated discussions from time to time.

The secret to a happy relationship is how you navigate through these disagreements to a feeling of resolution. This doesn't mean finding a solution; it means getting to the point where you both feel heard and empathized with. In the end we all need to feel respected, especially in the midst of disagreements.

Dr. Marshall Rosenberg developed a communication model called "nonviolent communication" or NVC. (Rosenberg uses the word "violence" in the broadest way, which includes *language that is disconnecting, blaming or judging*.) Nonviolent Communication is now taught all over the world in everything from international diplomacy to business mediation to parenting and intimate relationships. It all boils down to *relationship*, regardless of the form it takes. Human beings have needs, and if our needs aren't being met, we react; we pull away, fight back, or give up. We make so many mistakes in trying to get our needs met! Some of us may have been punished for expressing our needs, growing up to believe our needs are selfish.

If we're to understand our partner's needs, we must first understand our own. It's helpful to consider what our needs even are! Feel free to each write down your basic human needs on a piece of paper so you can review them altogether. Here are some examples to get you started:

Fundamental Needs: Shelter, food, water, money, exercise, safety

Personal Needs: Personal goals and dreams, morals, values, spirituality, fun, beauty, peace, creativity

Relational Needs: Trust, respect, empathy, vulnerability, support, acceptance

At some point in life, usually starting early on, some of our needs aren't met. This can leave us feeling wounded and particularly sensitive (when it comes to those needs). If you suddenly find yourself getting triggered, with your heart pounding and anger rising, it's likely that one of your "wounded" needs is being threatened. This is when voices grow louder and accusations start flying! If you manage to catch yourself in this crucial moment and consider the possible unmet needs underlying your or your partner's anger or sadness, you'll find a shortcut through the most painful part of a disagreement. If one of you can hold up the "time-out" sign with your hands — with the prior agreement that "time-out" means stop talking — you can both take a breath and apply some solid communication skills. You'll then have a chance to step out of the painful escalation and into a conversation that's productive and connecting.

Who doesn't want this? Seriously! If you can avoid painful arguments in your relationship, you can literally add years onto your life!

Applying NVC principles doesn't mean you're bypassing real conversation or sugarcoating real feelings; it means you're bringing discipline to your communication, so you can avoid painful patterns of conflict. It teaches you how to stay vulnerable, empathetic, and connected while expressing your feelings and needs. It's stepping out of the playground into *mature relating*.

Compassionate communication is not something we were taught in school or that was modeled at home (at least, not for most of us). If you were to witness how most couples handle conflict (which I witness often as a relationship coach), you'd see a lot of blaming, presumptions, accusations, talking over each other, and escalation that leads to wounding. A conversation about something as mundane as household chores can end in hurt and pain that drags on for days!

Nonviolent communication teaches us to handle conflict by following these eight steps.

1. State just the facts.

You start with the facts of what happened. Just the facts; no interpretation! The facts are what a video camera would capture, plain and simple. Agreeing on what happened factually starts you off on the right foot.

> **What to say**: "I told you we had to leave in five minutes and to lock the garage door. You agreed to do that. When I came back in three minutes you were not ready, and the garage door was still open". These are facts that you can both agree on. Start there.

> **What *not* to say**: "I asked you to do a simple thing, but you ignored it because you never listen. You never do what you say. You can't be trusted!" This is judgment and blaming and will put you both on the defense from the get-go.

2. Take turns talking.

Alternate speaking while the other listens *without commenting*. Arguments usually involve two people talking over each other with neither really listening. When we don't feel heard, it's infuriating, so set yourself up to both listen and be heard.

3. Show empathy.

Escalation happens when you don't feel heard. When you listen to your partner share their feelings, try making an empathetic statement to show them you understand what they're saying. Please understand that being empathetic doesn't mean you necessarily agree with their interpretation (of what happened); it simply acknowledges that you hear what they're saying and that you care about their feelings. Keep it simple and use some of their own language in your empathy statement. For example: "I know it's important for you to be on time for things. I'm sure it was frustrating for you to feel like I wasn't hearing you." You'll be surprised how quickly an argument will de-escalate when your partner hears your empathy statement. Their nervous system can relax, and solutions can be found.

4. Express your feelings.

Now that you've discussed the *facts* without interpretation, you can layer in *feelings* to the conversation. But here's the tricky part: you must do this without blaming or judging the other person. It's easy to use words that mix feelings with accusations, such as used, abused, betrayed, attacked, manipulated, neglected, rejected, or threatened. Instead, stay with feelings that don't underhandedly blame your partner; use words such as hurt, scared, sad, excited, irritated, confused, or surprised. These words will create connections instead of defensive reactions.

Many of us don't have a large vocabulary for feelings. You can search the internet for the term "The Feelings Wheel" and use it the next time you want to express your emotions.

Stay with "I" statements and away from "you" statements. When we're fighting with our partner, we'll often express our feelings by pointing the finger and making accusations, such as, "*You* make me feel neglected because *you* never listen to me, and *you* always make us late! And *you* don't care about our home." Instead, consider this approach: "When I saw that the garage door was still open, I felt frustrated that we might be late. I also felt afraid that our home wasn't going to be safe while we were away." You sense the difference in the emotional content, right? When our partner confesses their feelings without blaming or judging us, it gives us the space to step into their shoes, hear their feelings, and be open to finding a solution. There's no need to protect or defend ourselves.

5. Stay vulnerable.

Sometimes it's difficult to stay vulnerable in the middle of an argument. What does vulnerability look like at such times? It's not *defending* yourself. Nor is it *making excuses*. Instead, it means *owning up to your own shit!* Vulnerability isn't weakness, either, nor does it mean simply *giving in*. And it's not disempowering. Vulnerability means acknowledging our imperfections and being brave enough to show the genuine feelings beneath our overt anger, such as sadness, disappointment, or fear. These subsurface feelings usually run the show.

6. Express your needs.

Expressing your needs doesn't mean making demands or manipulating someone or strategizing to get your needs met. It means stating clearly and straight-forwardly the needs that aren't being met in the moment. Again, to use our example: "I have a need to be on time so people know they can count on me to be punctual. I also have a need to feel safe in my own home by making sure things are locked up before we leave."

7. Make a request.

In every disagreement, if certain needs aren't being met, we can still make a request to meet those needs. Often arguments leave us feeling upset and unclear on what steps will lead to a resolution. We could be so busy defending ourselves against blame and judgment that we overlook such a request. Consider what request you could make in such moments, so your partner understands your needs. For instance, you might ask the following: "Can we agree to try to walk out the door five minutes earlier than necessary, and I'll agree to trust that you'll try to be on time and keep our home safe?"

8. Agree on a future action to avoid this conflict next time.

I often see couples skip this final and important step in my office. If in the recounting of an argument I notice they've omitted what future agreement they're going to make to avoid the same conflict, I suggest they do it with me. It's usually a pretty obvious and doable agreement but saying it out loud helps you hold yourself accountable next time. It also communicates to our partner that both of you are moving forward with good intentions.

Look at them again or even write them down. The next time you find yourself in an escalating argument with your partner, remind yourself of the eight steps to Compassionate Communication:

1. State the facts without interpretation.
2. Take turns talking and listening without interrupting.
3. Be empathetic to create connection.
4. Add your feelings without blaming.
5. Stay vulnerable and own your shit.
6. Express your needs without manipulation.
7. Make a request without demanding.
8. Agree on a future action that will bypass this conflict next time.

25.

Fight Like a Ninja!
Eight Rules to "Fighting Well"

It's wonderful to spend time with the person we love, but sometimes a lot of exposure can put our relationship skills to the test. The person upon whom we rely for love and protection might push our buttons and cause us more stress than comfort! If there's one thing I've learned over many years coaching couples, it's that good relationships aren't created by chance or some magical starstruck union that was "meant to be." While they might start out like that, enduring good relationships happen because two people agree on "rules of engagement" during disagreements that will inevitably arise. And here's the takeaway; these rules and skills can be learned and taught.

Like any field of knowledge, couples therapy is always shifting and growing along with our cultural norms, yet certain rock-solid unchanging tools are known to help love and respect thrive. One of them is learning how to fight! That's right, I use the word "fight" because if you're in an intimate relationship with another human being, there will be fights. You can count on it!

We bring our *whole selves* into a relationship. That includes our own wounds and fears around conflict. Our upbringing and how we saw people fight around us influenced how we deal with conflict now. The good, the bad and the ugly of it. But it's never too late to change our unhealthy patterns of conflict and say "stop" to old programming that makes our fights horrible and hurtful.

I teach couples how to "fight" well in my private online coaching. Within three sessions, they transform their ability to face conflict, work through it, and return to connection. They're freed from the constant cycle of battling with their beloved, which only wears down intimacy and destroys sexual trust and connection.

I find it very rewarding to read their emails about how they applied their newly-learned fighting skills to real life conflict. Even when triggered, they remembered the agreements they made to move through arguments as a team. Acknowledge the inevitable: At some point you're both going to find yourselves getting triggered and gearing up for a fight. Your minds will start racing with accusations and judgments. Blood will start rushing to your head, and your heart will start pounding while your voices rise. Your "reptilian brain" will take over with the singular focus on *surviving*. At that point, what comes out of your mouth will no longer be rational, logical, or kind.

You'll find yourself (often within seconds) in "fight, flight, or freeze." Literally, you'll be run by your reptilian brain until you find your way to a calm state where your amygdala regains function. (Your wonderful amygdala is where all the rational, empathetic, compassionate, nurturing parts of you live.) Both parts of our brain — the reptilian and the amygdala — are designed to keep us alive. One by fighting, fleeing, or freezing; the other through connection, protection and support. Our Ninja power in conflict arises from being able to shift from our reptilian brain to our emotional brain.

Before I list some basic rules for you and your partner to agree to before you find yourselves gearing up for a showdown, bring awareness to the fact that you're starting to get triggered, and a fight is looming. Take a deep breath and stay committed to fighting like a Ninja! Don't freak out! And don't run away or attack. Remember that fighting is normal. The skill isn't learning to *never fight*; it's how quickly you move through the fight and back to connection.

Start to take some deep breaths. Breathing deeply is miraculous! It immediately calms our nervous system and lessens the experience of fight, flight, or freeze. It short-circuits our animal brain and reengages our emotional brain.

Take full responsibility for your own triggers and emotional reactions. It is a "lightbulb moment" for couples when they acknowledge that they are responsible for their own reactions and their own feelings. Until you can both stop pointing the finger and blaming, you won't be able to find resolution. Become aware of how you're contributing to the current conflict and speak from that place first.

Be willing to stay in the discomfort of conflict. This means don't blow off steam and escalate your anger with mean words and personal insults. Don't swear or raise your voice. Don't use violence or threats of violence. Don't make idle threats like "leaving the relationship" while in a triggered state. And don't go silent as a form of punishment. All of these things are ways we avoid the discomfort of disconnection. We run from it by throwing these hand grenades into the fire. Anger overrides the fear and sadness that resides just under the surface. Staying in the discomfort means assessing what's needed in order to de-escalate and communicate effectively, and trusting that by moving one step at a time you'll find your way back to connection.

Call for a time-out if needed. Step out of an escalation of angry words by taking a time-out. As I've suggested in previous chapters, you can ask for a time-out with words or you can simply put your hands up in a "T" shape, signaling to your partner that you need to take some space in order to collect your thoughts. Now let's be clear: A time-out doesn't mean stomping out and slamming the door behind you! It's saying to your partner that you need some space in order to collect your thoughts and de-escalate the energy that could lead to hurt feelings.

Tell them how long you'll be gone if you're leaving the room. Let them know what you're doing, like going for a walk or moving to another room in the house. Walking out without communicating these things just leaves your partner feeling abandoned, afraid, and stewing in their own resentment (for being walked out on).

Own your own shit. If you take a time-out, use that time to look at your part in the conflict. How did you contribute to the escalation? What could you have said or done differently? And be prepared to talk about those things when you come together again. *Nothing disarms a conflict quicker than one person stepping up and owning their part of it.* (Read that sentence over again!) Don't be afraid to be the first one to stop blaming and get real (and ask that your partner do the same).

Stop defending and listen deeply. No matter how angry we may feel in the moment, we can put ourselves in someone else's shoes, even if it's just for a few seconds. Genuinely listen to them and feel what it's like for them under the anger. Stop defending yourself for a moment and actually *listen*. And, as you look into your beloved partner's glaring face, remember this: *Within every angry emotion is a need not being met.* Ask yourself: What is the need that's not being met right now? What are they crying out for underneath the anger? What could you do or say *right now* that would help them connect to the suppressed feelings underlying their anger?

26.

Trauma:
Its Visible and Invisible Impact on Couples

> *"Trauma is not something that happened to you; trauma is what happens inside you, as a result of what happened to you."*
>
> — Dr. Gabor Maté, Trauma Expert

Dr. Gabor Maté is a respected author, speaker, and expert on trauma, addiction, and mental health. His work has served to open our eyes to the world-wide trauma epidemic, and his perspectives have helped us see more clearly the role trauma plays in addiction, suicide, and depression.

Statistically, 60 percent of men and 50 percent of women experience some form of trauma in their lives. It makes sense then that the relationships of nearly half my therapy couples are impacted by some form of personal trauma. Dr. Maté describes trauma as *a sane reaction to an insane situation*. It's the survival mechanism that steps in during periods of threat, to detach us from our feelings, and protect us from the "overwhelm" experienced in that moment. Just as we'd do what's necessary to heal a broken bone, so must we attend to the emotional wounds of trauma to live emotionally full and happy lives.

Healing trauma ultimately includes finding our way back to those forgotten feelings, acknowledging them, allowing ourselves to feel them, and addressing the initial wound with self-understanding. This is one area where a trained person can help guide you safely through the buried feelings.

Trauma can occur in both sudden, one-time events, or in repeated, ongoing physical and emotional wounding. We can experience trauma through negative belief systems and shame instilled in us by others, or trauma inherited through our lineage of ancestors. Early life trauma runs especially deep, given the vulnerable and susceptible state of a young child. Trauma is apparent in those who are obviously dysfunctional, as well as in the lives of seemingly high-functioning people. Trauma haunts the privileged as well as the underprivileged. It knows no income bracket, and where happiness is concerned, it affects all people indiscriminately.

Trauma itself is invisible to others. Like any mental condition, it's a subjective reality to the person who lives with it, and ultimately, it may arise and be witnessed in the container of a relationship. Trauma can show itself in our relationships in many ways:

- If we suffer from early life trauma, our capacity to emotionally attach to another will be hindered by insecurity or avoidance.
- The shame that often accompanies trauma can undermine our sexual self-confidence.
- Sexual trauma can create disassociation from our bodies and our partner.
- If our trauma is triggered, our reactions can be extreme and emotional.
- Suppressed anger and sadness settle in the body like armor, manifesting physical illness and emotional rigidity.
- Depression and disconnection make it hard to be emotionally intimate with another.

- We may use compulsion and addiction to self-soothe our pain, but this will push others away.
- If our trauma is based on betrayal, abandonment, or abuse, trust will be a challenge.

Everyone processes trauma differently. By becoming aware of the prevalence of trauma in our society, we can start to recognize the signs of trauma in our loved ones. We can acknowledge that our relationships are complex and that emotional challenges between two people are often born out of the personal, subjective battles within individuals. An individual's emotional capacity in relationships is based on a lifetime of experiences. Those who've experienced trauma may have disconnected from their feelings as a protective strategy. To grow in healthy relationships, we must express and share our feelings. A loving, trauma-aware partner within the structure of a trusted relationship can offer a place for healing to occur.

What can you do to support healing in your partner? If your relationship suffers from emotional obstructions, disassociation, and the numbness that comes from trauma, talk to your partner, and consider finding professional help to support healing.

What does healing look like in relationships? Trauma keeps our bodies in perpetual stress, ready to react to threats and protect ourselves, just as we did when the threat was real.

We have four automatic physiological reactions to an event that is perceived as stressful or frightening:

Fight: attacking, getting angry, yelling, fighting back

Flight: leaving, avoiding, withdrawing

Freeze: becoming silent, disassociating, immobility

Appease: doing or saying whatever is necessary to stop the threat

At the time of threat, we turn to these strategies to keep ourselves safe. Understanding these behaviors, when they arise in our relationships, as survival strategies in response to trauma creates compassion and patience for the inner battles our partner may be fighting in the moment. There are ways to help your partner feel safe:

- Listen to your partner without judgment. Express empathy and compassion to lower their stress hormones.
- Remember that consensual holding, touching, and cuddling calms their nervous system.
- Slow down and attune to your partner's needs during intimacy to help them avoid overwhelm and dissociation.
- Help them breathe deeply, move, dance, and play. These somatic tools release trauma in the body.
- Trust that trauma has its own intelligence and desire to heal. Support your partner's journey in discovering what that healing looks like for them.
- Help them find healthy ways to self-soothe in painful moments.

Educate yourself. Study the work of trauma experts and become knowledgeable about the kind of trauma your partner suffers. Become their teammate in seeking professional help, rather than becoming their doctor.

27.

Jealousy:
Taming the Beast

I once sat in on a group conversation about jealousy. The attendees were made up mostly of people in polyamorous and open relationships. For this group, jealousy is an emotion that requires honest investigation to successfully live their chosen relationship models. Those who choose to have multiple partners necessarily need to learn how to manage jealousy by working together with their partners to minimize it. It's not an easy task, but it's part of the territory if you want to step outside of the agreements that usually come with monogamy.

Alternative relationship models look at jealousy with fresh eyes. They acknowledge the complexity and challenge of this subject but approach it with a desire to deconstruct the destructive impacts jealousy can have. These couples talk about the challenges of jealousy openly; they set clear boundaries to help manage it, but most importantly they shine a bright light on an aspect of coupledom that usually lurks in the shadows, filled with judgment, shame, and conflict.

I consider relationship jealousy to be one of the more painful emotional challenges, regardless of your chosen relationship model. No one teaches us how to protect ourselves from the agonizing grip of jealousy. In full force, jealousy is emotionally (and physically) overwhelming. It not only cuts to our deepest fear of not being loved but, on a very primal level, jealousy is a warning sign that even our physical survival could be threatened (if we were to lose our partner to another).

If jealousy triggers the survival part of our brain into "fight or flight," it's understandable that jealousy can cause us to act from a highly stressed state of emotions such as anxiety, fear, and anger. It's also understandable that we may say and think things that don't reflect our "best selves." In a triggered state, we have no access to grounded logic or effective problem solving until we reengage our frontal cortex and regulate ourselves back into a calmer state of mind. Returning to emotional regulation may start by taking a more objective look at jealousy as a natural part of who we are based on our past experiences or wounding. Developing compassion for our feelings is the first step in calming our triggered instinctual brains.

Our core attachment wounds often play a big role in our experience of jealousy. Many subjective experiences can lead us to feel jealous:

- Depending on validation and feeling special
- Fearing being alone
- Seeing life through the eyes of loss and scarcity
- Comparing ourselves to others and doubting our own worth
- Being afraid of rejection and anxiously seeking belonging

(I'll add a caveat here that if you have good reason to be jealous based on real-life events such as infidelity or being lied to, then you and your partner have work ahead to repair that damage and build trust again. Many couples come through these ruptures with more honesty and intimacy than they had previously.)

If you acknowledge that jealousy strains your relationship, and you'd like to work as a team with your partner to manage it, here are some suggestions to start domesticating the beast.

Talk it out. The hardest thing to do is admit that you're jealous, without blaming your partner for making you feel that way. "I feel jealous right now. Can you help me through it?" It's a vulnerable confession that deserves a compassionate, undefended response. Help your partner feel safe enough to share their feelings and fears. Listen to the story they're telling themselves with compassion rather than defend yourself or immediately try to fix it. They may feel some shame in admitting their jealousy, but sharing their story and confessing their fears can help them feel heard, and sharing can calm their nervous system. Empathize with what they're feeling. If you've ever been jealous yourself, remember the pain of that emotion and put yourself in their shoes.

Reassure them. After they feel heard by you, consider what your partner might need to hear from you to help them find a healthy security in the relationship. What can you say to reassure them that you're on their side? Express your love and commitment to the relationship. Remind them of the strength of your relationship, your attraction to them, and your desire to honor your agreed-upon boundaries.

Remember your agreements. When you're both in a calm state of mind, sit down and talk about your agreements and the boundaries in your relationship. Some couples bypass this conversation, assuming their partner should just know what is and isn't appropriate. Don't assume you're on the same page. Every relationship is unique and talking about how you conduct yourself around others is the only way you can discover what helps your partner's sense of security. If you're a *people pleaser* you may find yourself over-extending your agreements to appease their discomfort, so be honest and trust that your relationship is strong enough to hold the truth!

Build trust. Trust is both given in good faith and earned over time. Our reassuring words are helpful in a challenging moment, but our actions are what lay the foundation for real trust. Keep your word. Do what you say you'll do. Agreements aren't written in stone; they can be changed if one or both of you feel the need for change. However, breaking agreements without conversation or consent can cause a rupture. Stay current and honest with your needs and work as a team to support each other's sense of security in the relationship. Of course, this applies to any relationship model, whether it's an open or closed relationship, agreements matter.

If you feel like you're in a good place together, sit down and have a conversation about jealousy. Acknowledge the pain of jealousy and share the impact it's had in your life. Perhaps you don't see yourself as a jealous person, in which case this subject may not hold any charge for you. If so, work extra hard to stay empathetic with a partner who does identify as jealous. We all have our beasts to battle on occasion, and being there to support our partner on the front lines is what a good relationship is all about.

28.

Slow Down! Couples at Play: Playful Lessons from Burning Man

My partner and I returned from the festival feeling enlivened, enriched, and exhausted. Every year we embrace the challenge that comes with high heat, dust storms, and late nights, as part of the week-long, fully immersive experience in the middle of the Nevada Desert known as "Burning Man."

What brings tens of thousands to this uninhabitable place every year? I believe it's the desire to play again, with the same spirit and wonder we did as children!

Most of Burning Man's long-held principles lend themselves to *play* by promoting cooperation, inclusion, radical self-expression, generosity, and open-hearted presence — all the elements of life with which every one of us is born and that we intuitively understand as children. Play is a reset button for our over-stressed, news-saturated, time-pressured adult minds.

Most couples I work with will readily admit that play is not something they experience on a regular basis. Life has become too busy. There's barely enough time to be alone to talk, much less play! Our time has become more about schedules, finances, work, family, and errands. We wake up planning our busy days and fall into bed drained. One of the casualties of growing up is our ability to embrace play for its own sake, to seek out joyful moments for no other reason than to be present in the moment and have fun together.

Playing on the Playa

One of our neighbors on the playa (meaning 'beach' in Spanish) was a couple in their early fifties who are parents of three kids in college. When I asked if they ever bring their kids to Burning Man, they said no; Burning Man is their time to be together and enjoy an adventure as a couple. They looked and acted more as they did at the age when they met, twenty years ago. They dressed in colorful outfits that expressed their playful sides and laid-back attitudes. Burning Man was their annual escape to reconnect, having nothing more to do than be together in a mood of exploration and adventure. Each day we'd watch them hop on their bikes and head off, returning late into the night with smiles and stories to share.

When couples give each other permission to play together, they acknowledge that their relationship is a place to engage their imaginations and embrace parts of themselves they may have left behind along the way. Play for its own sake is not a trivial, unnecessary activity. *Play is foundational to maintaining a happy, growing relationship.* (Read that sentence again, out loud!) When we invite joyful, carefree moments into our time with our partner, we experience the childlike essence behind the busy adult, and the inherent joy in living with which every one of us is born.

If the idea of play seems like a distant memory in your relationship, maybe it's time to sit down and talk about it! What activities would bring out playfulness in you as a couple? Is it learning how to partner dance? Or sharing a new sport? Is it hitting the road to commune with nature? Is it camping around a fire with friends? Or laughing together at a local comedy club? Is it starting a 2000-piece puzzle? Or pulling out a Jenga tower?

Of course, we can bring play into the bedroom as well, using our imagination to explore our erotic personas and engage with our partner through a different lens. Couples who enjoy roleplay appreciate the experience of stepping out of the norm and embracing alternative ways of relating to each other erotically. (*More on that later in the Sex section of this book.*)

A few years ago a client of mine discovered a side of herself that loved to pretend she was still in college, before the kids, the job, and the mortgage payments. She gave that part of her the name *Sassy*. Her partner loved spending time with Sassy. When she brought Sassy out to play, her partner felt invited into a more carefree space as well. Sassy was the signal that conversations about adult worries were put on hold, and *play* was the focus.

Bringing play into your relationship is a team effort. In order to let ourselves feel playful, we need to feel supported by our partner. We can give each other permission to make the great escape from adult demands.

- Trust that your partner has your back in new adventures. Be patient with each other as you try out new ways of being playful together.
- Be courageous by stepping into your more child-like enthusiasm. out of your adult responsibilities and let go into a more child-like enjoyment.
- Attune to your partner, to create a shared experience.
- Collaborate in designing the play that you're creating together.

Cooperate to bring that vision into being, whether that's riding your bikes through the sights and sounds of Burning Man, planning a vacation full of new experiences, or sneaking off for a night in a hotel room with tickets to your favorite live concert.

One of the challenges of creating play at Burning Man was trying to set up camp during two days of winds and dust storms. I have memories of holding onto the end of a 15-foot square tarp, trying not to be swept off my feet with gusts of 30 mph winds. By the end of that day, we lay exhausted, laughing about what we had to overcome to get settled, and feeling unified in our shared victory.

Be happy; nothing is in control

Playfulness requires full participation and presence, requiring us to relinquish the control we cling to in our day-to-day lives. Play can push us out of the comfort zone of familiarity. It asks us to put our phones down and forget about timelines. Play challenges our rigid, adult expectations of *right* and *wrong*, or *yes* and *no*.

One of the most important transitions I make at Burning Man usually comes within the first three days, when I'm confronted with my need to control circumstances and surroundings. It's in that confrontation where the true reset can begin. Letting go of control and going with the flow is the gift that play gives us.

There's a science behind play. It's been shown to release endorphins and improve brain functionality. It stimulates creativity and, of course, increases our feelings of well-being. New forms of play introduce into our relationships the much-needed experiences of novelty and mystery, two of the necessary ingredients for a vibrant, growing relationship. When a couple engages in the novelty of new experiences, their brains produce all the love hormones that support bonding and closeness.

Oxytocin comes from the attraction of seeing our partner with fresh eyes as we engage in new experiences that bring out their joyfulness.

Vasopressin helps us mobilize physically and emotionally to take on new adventures.

Phenylethylamine is another love hormone responsible for releasing adrenaline that comes from new experiences.

Dopamine comes from the bonding and closeness of sharing those new experiences.

All these love hormones combine to make a cocktail of powerful feelings. In other words, when we introduce novel ways of playing together, Mother Nature supplies us with everything we need to feel happy and in love with our partner.

New experiences can be as simple as trying out indoor rock climbing, visiting an Escape Room, or jumping on a local zip line in the woods. If a couple comes to see me complaining of low desire or boredom, we talk about the importance of keeping *novelty* and *mystery* alive in their relationship. These two ingredients help produce the chemical soup that reawakens desire between partners. Sit down with your partner and talk about what play means in your relationship. Take a break from this crazy adult world. You can be sure it'll be here when you get back from your personal playground, feeling renewed, engaged, and happily exhausted.

BOOK TWO:
TURN UP

In this section we look at the often-mysterious world of desire, how to turn up your own desires, and how to confidently express those desires to your partner. You'll discover the importance of self-awareness, open communication, and the delicate art of sexual initiation. Through practical guidance and reflective exercises, let's explore how to turn up desire with authenticity, empathy, and vulnerability.

29.

From Drought to Desire:
Seven Steps Out of Inertia

No matter how dry your sex life is right now, there's a path forward for you as a couple. Like anything in nature, change is constant; everything has an ebb and flow, an expansion and contraction, a rising and falling. Yet when it comes to sex and intimacy, ebbs and flows leave us feeling confounded and insecure.

If you asked 100 couples if they've ever been through a sexual drought, 90 percent of them would say "yes." Children, travel, sickness, stress, distance, and hormones all play their part in reducing sexual frequency. Based on this 90 percent statistic, you could almost say that it's *expected* that in a long-term relationship sex will wane, at least for periods of time.

Why then do so many couples get broadsided when their sexual frequency drops off?

First, we equate a sexual drought with a broken relationship. Second, no one prepares us for it or gives us solid advice to move out of a drought. When sex becomes very infrequent or nonexistent for periods of time, our fears and insecurities get the best of us. We build negative stories around our situation and imagine the worst. Next, we do what most of us do when it comes to sex: *we don't talk about it.*

Our stories might be something like:

- *My partner doesn't find me attractive anymore.*
- *My desires don't matter.*
- *Sex goes away in most long-term relationships.*
- *My partner is interested in someone else.*
- *My partner doesn't love me like that anymore.*
- *This is the first step toward separation or divorce.*

These are devastating stories we tell ourselves, leaving us feeling hopeless, resentful, afraid, and unworthy. Our internal negative stories fuel the emotional divide. Ironically, our stories erode the very intimacy and connection that lay the foundation for sex to happen. Unless we learn to talk about sex openly and honestly, without blame or projection, we can slip into sexual inertia.

And here's the thing... Nature has an indisputable law when it comes to inertia, which is:

Objects remains at rest, or in uniform motion in the same straight line,
unless acted upon by some external force.

A sexual drought is a form of inertia, and unless some external force acts upon it, it will remain *as is.*

So you need to apply some external forces to shift this sexual inertia. The first and foremost external force is the simple act of *acknowledgement.* A couple should sit down together and acknowledge that their sex life is in a state of inertia. They can then ask each other (and themselves) how they feel about that fact. Keep in mind that there's no right or wrong when it comes to sexual frequency. If both partners are content with less sex, but enjoy it when it happens, then that's the right frequency for them. Every relationship is unique. If both partners agree that they want the frequency to change, this is the matter to explore. This is where you can come together as a team and share your thoughts, with one caveat: No blaming or finger pointing allowed!

Stay curious as to what derailed your sex life. Was it the birth of your second child? Was it family stress? Career pressure?

If the cause of inertia is related to the *quality* of sex rather than the *quantity*, then a different conversation needs to happen. (And this is where some coaching could help.) If you both agree that more frequent sex is important for your relationship, follow these seven steps:

> **Step 1**: Acknowledge the origin of your shift in sexual frequency, and the reality that sexual inertia has set in. Remember the 90 percent; you're not alone or broken.

> **Step 2**: Share your feelings about it without blaming your partner. For example, you could say, "I miss being with you sexually. I miss feeling close to you." Or "I'd love to work together to make sex a priority in our lives again!" There are lots of loving, romantic, and appreciative ways to tell your partner you miss sex. Let them hear it.

> **Step 3**: Agree to re-approach sex gradually, if it's been a bit of a hiatus. Start with nonsexual touching. Many couples end up avoiding any kind of touch, if they're in a sexual drought. Connect in simple ways like walking arm-in-arm, dancing, or engaging in partner yoga. Rediscover your natural polarity. Exercise and breathe together. Start to get intimate again with each other's bodies, without any sexual goal, and enjoy the journey of sensual touch and massage to awaken desire.

Step 4: Returning to sex after some time away can be awkward. Just agree that awkwardness might be part of your experience. Once you acknowledge it, it's less intimidating and can even be humorous. Be patient as you both start to rediscover some ease and flow in your sexuality. Don't worry, you'll get there!

Step 5: Come to an agreement on your preferred sexual frequency. Remember, a willing, enthusiastic partner creates the kind of quality sex that makes up for quantity. If there's a discrepancy in frequency, meet in the middle. Putting pressure on a partner to have sex with you is not sexy and fuels the divide.

Step 6: Make an agreement with each other that if you notice your sex life starting to dry up again, you'll both acknowledge it and nip it in the bud while keeping these seven steps in mind. Don't create stories that fuel your discontent! Talking honestly about sex can be as easy as talking about lunch. Let go of defensiveness and negative presumptions. Sex is a natural part of an intimate relationship that requires attention and awareness. Treat it that way.

Step 7: Going forward, prioritize sex by planning sex. Make a date and keep your promise to show up with full presence. Couples who plan their sex dates are far more likely to avoid the slippery slope back into a state of drought.

If sexual inertia is paying a visit, come together as a team and decide what external force you're going to introduce in order to shift out of the state of rest and back into the state of play.

30.

Mismatched Desire:
The Number One Challenge!

Mismatched desire is the number one challenge my clients bring to me for resolution. Let's discuss how to fix it!

"We don't have sex anymore. I don't understand why."

These clients don't feel wanted or desired. And they don't know what to do about it. It usually starts with accusations that it's *their partner's fault*. They blame their lack of sex on their partner's loss of desire and interest. (It goes without saying that this applies to both genders, but here I'll speak about the male perspective from my coaching practice.)

There's a common progression in this scenario. After some weeks, months, or even years of initiating sex without feeling any desire reflected back to them, these men get to the point of no longer asking. They find their own ways to avoid sex and begin shutting down emotionally. Resentment sets in and creates an undercurrent of withholding and tension in the relationship. This shows itself as irritability, angry outbursts, or passive aggressive behavior, all of which undermine intimacy and attraction — the very thing for which they long.

One of my first questions is, "Have you had an honest and open conversation about your sex life and why your partner doesn't want to have sex anymore?"

"No," is the typical answer.

"Why not?" I'll ask them.

"Because I know why. They're not interested in sex anymore."

Sometimes the hardest part of sex is talking about it in a way that's curious, open, and solution focused. For that to happen these men need to move beyond their sense of [*fill in the blank: betrayal, sadness, punishment, withholding*]. These feelings are understandable. It's scary to lose your partner's desire. *What if they're not attracted to me anymore? What if they've found someone else they desire? What if we never get our sex life back again? What if our relationship is over?* It becomes a rabbit hole of "what ifs" that goes deeper and deeper into subjective despair, shame, and resentment.

With this mindset, these men can turn to affairs or pornography as their primary sexual outlet, leaving their partner feeling abandoned and alone. Shame becomes part of both partner's stories. He has shame because he no longer feels desired by the person he loves, and his partner feels shame because she knows she's not meeting the needs of the person she loves. Shame is isolating. It thrives in silence. It eats away at our self-esteem and tells us we're unlovable. Couples end up arguing about porn consumption or promiscuity instead of what's happening in their sex life. It's easier to point the finger at the symptoms than to speak honestly about the source of the problem: desire.

Thankfully, there's a way out of this rabbit hole that starts with an honest and vulnerable dialogue. That means no blaming, no defending, no presumptions, no accusations! Discussing sexual challenges is one of the most vulnerable conversations we can have with our partner. Learn the tools to become effective communicators, compassionate listeners, and more curious friends and partners.

31.

Desire:
The Missing Link

What drives committed long-term partners to seek out affairs? Is it the desire for a specific person? A need for more sexual fulfillment? What are they not getting at home that moves a person to look elsewhere?

The clients I've had over the years who looked for sex outside of their relationship often confess that their affair validated their *desirability*. Feeling *desirable* was missing from their relationship. They lost the sense of themselves as an autonomous sexually desirable person; engaging with a new partner was the fast route to get that back (or so they hoped).

Feeling desired is often the part of our sexual experience that gets lost in long-term relationships. We can become better lovers, more sensitive listeners, more generous givers, even more desirous lovers ourselves, but if we don't *feel desired*, that missing piece can leave a painful void in our sexual experience.

Let's acknowledge that we all have a deep need to feel desired. The partner who most often initiates may *lead* with desire but may not *feel* desired. I can't count the number of initiating partners who've expressed their need to feel desired and come to coaching feeling depleted (from getting nothing back in return). Likewise, desire is important to the noninitiating partners. Even if their response is "no" to their partner's sexual initiation, they'll confess that if their partner stops initiating, they miss the feeling of being desired. They're the first to admit they take their partner's desire for granted. The tension that comes from the push-and-pull dynamic is suddenly replaced with the question, "Why doesn't my partner initiate anymore? Have they lost their desire for me?"

Feeling desire from a distance

Nature teaches us the necessity of ebb and flow. The tide flows in and then it flows out. The sun rises and then it sets. The summer's heat is followed by the winter's chill. This natural law of coming and going plays out in relationships as well. As children we navigate between the need to hang on to our parent's pant leg for security, and the longing to step away from what's secure. We let go of the pant leg in order to seek adventure and independence. This is where we form our secure or insecure attachment styles to other human beings. This natural stage of human development shows up in our intimate relationships as well. Partners often learn (the hard way) the necessary balance between merging and distancing, and the pitfalls of having too much of one without the other. *Merging* supports feelings of security, bonding, and familiarity. Counterintuitively, *distancing* supports mystery, passion and desire.

Without individuation, we would be cuddled up in jammies enjoying all the good feelings that come with togetherness while feeling none of the juice that comes with having enough distance from our partner for desire to come onboard. Every couple can assess the truth of this in their relationship and consider together the things they can do to support individuation. This doesn't need to be separate vacations; it could be as simple as solo walks, retreating behind a closed door with a good book, or spending time with separate friends. When we acknowledge the downsides of merging, we can welcome the upsides of individuation.

Here are some other things to keep in mind as you consider how to rekindle desire in your relationship:

We become what our partner sees: When our partner shows us their desire, we see ourselves through their eyes. Their vision of us empowers us to become the person they see us as: someone who's sexually desirable, attractive, and worthy of pursuit. We see ourselves through the eyes of their desire and, in turn, connect to our own desire.

You deserve to be a little selfish (in a good way): Desire is selfish in a way that says "I deserve to have desires. I deserve to seek out pleasure." Desire isn't focused on being of service. It's not caregiving someone else's experience. Having *your* desires is one way we express individuation in our relationship. Desire is a self-focused experience that's born from the promise of personal pleasure. It says, "I want you. You turn me on." It's that healthy selfishness that ignites feelings of passion and heightens the sexual polarity of taking and being taken.

Our partner's desire invites us into our own desire: When we feel our partner's empowerment to step into their desire, we're granted permission to claim our own assertiveness and boldness and lose ourselves in our own pleasurable experience. Our partner's expression of desire reminds us to follow our own bliss and embrace the freedom to feel and express our own desire. Our partner fuels our desire, and in return our desire fuels theirs. We create a self-generating circuit of energy exchange.

Sexual shame dampens desire: Sexual shame can be implanted in our brains through many experiences like

- being scolded for touching ourselves as young children;
- something inappropriate happening to us about which we feel conflicted;
- being exposed to sexual shame within our families; and
- sensing our partner's disapproval of our innate sexual desires.

Our parents, our peers, and our partners can all inflict shame on us in overt and subtle ways. We want to welcome our desire and let it flow from a place of self-acceptance. Accepting our desires requires the healing of any shame we've been carrying with us in our lives.

Feeling desire isn't always showing desire: Your partner isn't going to know you feel desire if you aren't able to show it. Learn what it's like to *show* your desire in very clear, confident, and direct ways. Sometimes it takes practice showing your desire! If you're shy, roleplay desire for your partner to get you started. Crawl to them across the floor like a cat in heat! Explore facial expressions that say, "I want you!" Touch them with intention and speak to them with a voice of seduction. Desire is a feeling to be expressed and experienced. Ask your partner for feedback as you find your authentic expression.

Use your largest sex organ to manufacture desire: Fantasy is one of the ways we can support desire and step out of the numbing familiarity that seems inevitable in long-term relationships. One couple I've coached used the fantasy of having another woman in their lives to create some mystery and novelty. By playing in the mind realm, we can safely explore scenarios that allow us to see our partner in more novel ways. Practice sharing your fantasies!

Authentic desire is not an act we perform: For desire to be authentic, it needs to be driven by what authentically turns us on.

Whether it's being swept up in a romantic embrace, or getting lost in transcendent union, or being pinned to the wall and ravished, our desires are unique to our true erotic nature.

Desire is one of life's great experiences. Desire motivates us and inspires our imagination. Desire identifies our wants and needs. It's not reserved for the young or limited to new relationships. Not feeling desirable, sexual shame, differing attachment styles, suppressed individuation, fear of showing desire — these are just a few of the challenges that can keep your desire hidden and unexpressed. These themes are common in my work with couples. 'Tis a tale as old as time!

32.

Naked and Afraid:
Seven Stress Busters for Your Bedroom

If you're wondering where your sex drive has gone, you're not alone. Sex and stress do not make happy bedmates. That's a biological fact. Human suffering, illness, politics, environmental issues, human rights violations, and finances are just some of our stressors. Bad news often comes at us from all directions; conversations with family and friends inevitably end up processing that bad news. Even in our happy moments, the undercurrent of stress may always be present.

Biologically, stress is killing our sex drives. Our emotional and physical stress is activating our "fight or flight" reflex, which reduces blood flow to our genitals. The release of the hormones cortisol and adrenaline depresses testosterone levels. A reduction in the neurotransmitters that produce feelings of well-being increases our risk of depression and anxiety. This all undermines erections and orgasms.

Researchers with the Massachusetts Male Aging Study — in an ongoing investigation of 1,709 people — concluded that men who suffer from stress are almost twice as likely to experience E.D. (erectile dysfunction). Stressed-out men shut down around sex.

Our bodies are not designed to encourage sexual thoughts when our brains are communicating that we may be in danger. We can't convince our bodies that we're safe, when in fact we're not. Unfortunately, we can't just reason ourselves out of being in fight or flight mode. Our bodies were built for stress: stress warns us of danger; it helps keep us alive. But our bodies were not built to live with ongoing high stress levels. We may not be able to avoid stress, but we can learn to manage it, and not let it regulate our sexual desires.

Here are some things to do to step off the stress wheel regularly and signal to your body that it's safe to relax for a while and turn your attention to what's pleasurable. (Print this out. Put it on your fridge. Remind yourself every day that you can choose to lower your stress levels regularly.)

Stress buster 1: Tell it like it is

Acknowledging that stress is at war with our sexual desire is the first step to lighten the load of our judgment of ourselves and each other. Sit down and have a conversation with your partner about your current sexual frequency. Share how stress impacts your sexual desire and reassure your partner that your loss of desire has nothing to do with them personally. Don't assume they know this. We all need to be reminded that we're sexually desirable and loved. Words go a long way to calm insecurities when it comes to sex.

Stress buster 2: Plan time for sex

I can't say this enough. Don't get stuck in the rut of letting the days go by hoping you or your partner will be in the mood to initiate intimacy. Agree that sex is important enough to prioritize. Put yourself in the room and trust that your initial resistance will fade as you start to slow down, breathe deeply and connect. Rather than making intercourse your goal, be open to whatever your intimate time together will bring. Just agree that for a set period of time your bodies will be in contact, one way or another. Touch, massage, hug, cradle, share. Make intimacy your goal, and everything else will follow.

Stress buster 3: Touch and be touched

Don't be afraid to ask for what you want from your partner. Ask for a massage or a shoulder rub or an extended hug. Offer to give one in return with no strings attached. Being in close proximity to our lover's body produces a host of feel-good hormones. Take advantage of it and get up close.

Stress buster 4: Orgasms are powerful

The one-step solution to stress? Give yourself an orgasm. Orgasms flood our brains with oxytocin. They are nature's antidote to high levels of cortisol, and that's why masturbation is such a common sleep aid. We now understand the profound impact orgasms have on our mental/ emotional state. Whether you're alone or with a partner, orgasms are abundant and free. Include them in your wellness practice as a sure-fire way to lower your stress levels and keep your sexual energy flowing.

Stress buster 5: Exercise daily

We all know how good it feels to know we're giving our body what it needs to be healthy and vital. While sex and stress don't jive, sex and exercise make a great pair. Move your body daily. You'll sleep better and your stress levels will drop. Use a brisk walk or run to prepare for intimacy and get your blood flowing to all the right places.

Stress buster 6: Stop, look, and listen

If you need a quick fix for the stress of a busy mind, use your five senses to drag your attention out of your chronic thinking and into your physical experiences. Our five senses; sight, smell, taste, touch and hearing are constantly feeding us present-time information. They show us what's beautiful, what smells good, what feels good against our skin, what tastes delicious. The problem is we're usually just not *listening*. We're stuck in past or future thoughts.

It takes a nanosecond to notice that your mind is somewhere other than where you are, and another nanosecond to drop your attention into your body where you actually live and breathe. Your body is where you experience pleasure, so tune in to your senses and enjoy what your body is telling you.

Stress Buster 7: Laugh therapy

Laughter and sex have a lot in common: they both strengthen neural pathways in the brain, building a feeling of closeness in a relationship. They support intimacy and connection with our partner by flooding our brains with dopamine. When we laugh, we can literally feel the stress leave our body. Our state is instantly changed. So, look for humor throughout your day. It may not always be obvious but it's there, waiting to be shared. Put on a favorite stand-up act, watch a comedy on Netflix, laugh out loud together, and let the good times roll... right into the bedroom.

33.

Rediscovering the Spark: Unleashing the Power of Polarity in Your Relationship

What is *polarity*?

Equal and opposite energies are found in every part of nature. Cause and effect, Yin and Yang, masculine and feminine, the initiating and the yielding, giving and receiving, leading and following, light and dark, heaven and earth — each opposite plays its role in forming the whole. Most of us flow easily between these roles. One moment we're following someone's lead in conversation or agreeing to someone else's plans for dinner, and the next we're giving directives to the babysitter or describing how we want our meal prepared in a restaurant.

When we stand in line for our morning coffee, we're guided to do what is necessary to get our coffee. When we give our coffee order, we're guiding the barista in how to make a coffee that pleases us. Neither you nor the barista is superior to the other. You're equal parts in an overarching mutual agreement to meet both of your needs: you get your coffee and she gets her paycheck. Unless there's a noted undercurrent of attraction between you and the barista, this isn't an *erotically* charged instance of polarity, unlike the polarity of leading and following that's inherent in a romantic relationship.

Polarity & passion

Polarity is necessary in keeping passion alive. It's the yin and yang of a union, reflecting the opposite and equal energies found everywhere in our natural world and cosmos. Polarity magnetically draws opposing sides toward the creation of a whole. Neither side is superior or more powerful; the equal and opposite male and female aspects of our human nature reside in all of us.

Couples who have discovered their authentic sexual polarity will often

- maintain that erotic spark outside of the bedroom;
- tend to see each other through "lover's eyes";
- tease and flirt with each other in the midst of their day;
- more easily locate their desire and show it to their partner, making them feel wanted and appreciated;
- share a lingering kiss, a sensual embrace or a loving squeeze of the butt;
- text sexy thoughts from the office in anticipation of a planned playdate; and
- enjoy high degrees of sexual confidence.

And if you're familiar with Dr. Sue Johnson's attachment style teachings, they'll both experience the *secure attachment* a strong connection brings.

A couple *lacking* polarity might describe their relationship by saying:

- "I feel like we've become more roommates than lovers,"
- "Neither of us feel motivated to be sexual anymore,"
- "It's easier to just watch TV and cuddle than it is to have sex,"

- "Our relationship has become platonic, like we're brother and sister,"
- "We know everything there is to know about each other. There's no mystery,"
- "We have sex but it feels awkward and stilted,"
- "We both want to initiate so we're trying to please each other at the same time," or
- "We both want to be seduced so neither of us will initiate something."

I often hear couples describe their partner as their *best friend*. On the surface this sounds idyllic. But what you gain in partnering with your *best friend* you lose in the sexual dynamic that creates desire, lustful anticipation for erotic escapes, and the excitement of viewing your partner through a lover's lens. Without the polarity of opposites, couples can settle into a sameness that creates comfort, security, and an intimacy that feels almost *familial*. Sooner or later, attraction is replaced with a brotherly or sisterly relating that can deaden the spark of desire or at least give it a back seat in intimacy. What was once sexual attraction coming from equal and opposite energies now feels unmotivated and predictable, lacking the tension of the polar pull. When it comes to sex, sameness does not create the erotic friction that makes passion come alive. Sexual polarity thrives in the play of opposites: leader and follower, pursuer and pursued, directive masculine energy and receptive feminine energy.

Masculine vs feminine energy

Gender has little to do with polarity. Everyone, regardless of gender, embodies masculine/yang energy and feminine/yin energy. As we slowly chip away at society's gender biases, we're learning to identify where we fall on the broad spectrum of masculine and feminine energy. Finding balance within our inherent masculine/feminine energy helps partners recognize and accept how to support polarity within themselves and in their relationship. The more we understand who we are energetically, the more we can loosen the grip of gender stereotypes that don't necessarily reflect our experience.

For example, the CEO who spends their days in a masculine, directive role may long to relinquish control and be told what to do. The nurturer who spends their days in a more feminine energy, taking care of and submitting to the requests of others, may long to take the reins and be in charge. When we accept who we authentically are on the scale of masculine and feminine energy, we start to understand our own internal polarity. We can then explore how polarity can shift the dynamic in our relationship.

Your authentic path to polarity: A case study

When Brad and Jenna came to see me for their first coaching session, they expressed the number one most common complaint I hear from long-term couples: They'd lost sexual desire and attraction. They both felt it was Brad's problem. Jenna wanted Brad to be more assertive with her in the bedroom. And Brad had no idea how to invoke the kind of energy Jenna needed. Because of this disconnect, sex had become routine and predictably unsatisfying. They were often left in the void of what was missing, and the silent disappointment that it might never change.

This led to resentment that impacted other parts of their relationship. It strained their patience with each other's shortcomings. Bickering became a daily routine.

Jenna found her attention drifting to men who embodied the kind of energy she was missing in Brad. She confessed to me that she felt dangerously close to secretly seeking that energy outside of the relationship. Jenna's work as a lawyer required her to be solidly planted in her masculine energy. When she got home from work, she brought that same level of directive energy to her family life, and her relationship. She felt the need to call the shots, make the decisions, and lead the way.

It didn't take me long to observe that Jenna's own masculine energy was preventing Brad from finding his own masculine energy in the relationship. As long as she was taking the reins in and out of the bedroom, Brad was inclined to assume the polar role with a more submissive demeanor of wanting to please and be of service. You can see where this led: This only solidified Jenna's own need to be in the directive role and undermined her respect for Brad. Their relationship had polarity but not in a way that served them.

The shift back to polarity for Jenna and Brad didn't happen on just a conceptual level: it came about through somatic exercises that connected both to parts of themselves that had gone dormant. By playing with erotic power through tools such as archetypes, physical experiencing, and roleplay, they found their polarities beginning to shift. As Jenna relaxed the more masculine energy she needed in her work environment — and felt safe enough to embody her more feminine side at home — she stopped focusing on Brad's deficits and began to trust his decisions and directives. In turn, Brad began to embrace his own sexual desire for his own pleasure rather than the need to please Jenna. This strengthened his capacity to confidently take charge. Jenna could let go and enjoy being ravished by Brad, while Brad was being fed by her receptivity and desire. They found a dynamic that fueled their desire and the attraction of opposing energies.

In time, their undercurrent of resentment and daily competition made way for an appreciation and respect for each other's new roles. They learned that it's not about trying to become someone other than their true selves but rather connecting with parts of themselves they'd abandoned over the years.

In conclusion, we all embody both masculine and feminine energy. Today we accept that gender is no longer a strictly binary concept, but rather a broad spectrum of energies. When we accept our place on this spectrum of masculine/feminine energy we can explore different sides of ourselves in relationship to our partners. While unhealthy relationship dynamics are formed unconsciously, healthy dynamics can be formed with *intention*. What is the dance of polarity in your relationship? Are you in the flow of your dance, or are you stepping on each other's toes?

34.

The Art of Sexual Initiation (Part 1): Putting Your Ducks in a Row

When I was nineteen years old, I wandered into a tiny antique shop in downtown Toronto, Canada. It was cluttered with a wide assortment of international knickknacks, worn carpets, and furniture in need of restoration. An old Japanese man sat in the corner working on an ink painting. When he saw me staring at a pair of wooden ducks high up on a shelf, he asked me if I knew about how these wooden ducks were traditionally used by married couples in Japan.

I deciphered from his broken English that usually the ducks sat facing in opposite directions in a home. If the woman was interested in sex that night, she would place the ducks facing each other. When the man came home at the end of the day, he'd check the ducks to get a read on her interest in being intimate. No words needed to be exchanged, no long conversations had to take place. The ducks facilitated what many couples struggle with: the comfort to talk about sex.

What the old Japanese man shared stuck with me over the decades. It was the first time I thought about creative ways of expressing desire and initiating sex. Clearly, the decision to use ducks to initiate sex began as a solution to a problem — a problem that was, no doubt, causing friction in relationships in Japan around the discomfort of talking about sex.

If you find it difficult to talk openly and honestly about sex with your partner, initiation is going to be an ongoing challenge. I suppose you could buy yourselves a pair of wooden ducks, but wouldn't it be better to transform your conversations about this subject?

Initiating sex is a mixed bag for couples. It comes with ease for some, where just a look or an innuendo sets things in motion, but for most couples, initiation is laden with a dynamic that creates feelings of frustration, misunderstanding, and resentment. If we're going to tackle this emotionally complex issue, we need to tune in to our partner, step out of defensive positions, and share our feelings and experiences. This opens us to empathy and connection. The "higher-desire" partner and the "lower-desire" partner can bridge the chasm of silence.

Partners tend to get lost in their own emotional experience. I view every couple as a unique puzzle to be pieced together based on their sexual histories and how those histories combine. It's helpful to see the complexity of emotions on both sides. The higher-desire person is often the one to initiate, believing that if they didn't, sex would never happen. If there's a pattern of their initiations being refused, they habitually brace themselves for disappointment, which undermines the energy of confidence and seduction. The lower-desire partner is the one being pursued. They hold the power in that moment to say "yes" or "no." It's a depolarizing position for both. This "yes or no" question flattens the energy of seduction, and the lower-desire partner will find all the reasons why sex, in that moment, doesn't work for them. At this point their answer will default to a "no." This dynamic kills desire for multiple reasons.

Let's unpack this exchange by looking at the feelings involved for both partners. If the higher-desire partner is the one to initiate and is often refused, they can end up feeling

- alone as the only one who is interested in making sex happen;
- shameful about their desires;
- disempowered in the relationship, in and out of the bedroom;
- resentful toward their partner who holds the power;
- judged for their sexual expectations;
- sad that their sexuality has no place for expression;
- unloved and undesired by their partner; and/or
- doubtful that they're worthy of a life that includes desire and affection.

If the lower-desire person is always the one being pursued, they could end up spending more time assessing their answer rather than locating their own desire. When they default to a "no," this often leaves them feeling

- guilty about always being the one to say no, knowing they're not meeting their partner's needs for sex and intimacy;
- pressured to meet their partner's needs in the moment;
- misunderstood when it comes to their needs, and what might work better for them;
- broken, believing there's something wrong with their sexuality;
- resistant in their bodies, which can appear as tension, contraction, or numbness;
- defended about trying to stay true to their preferences in that moment;
- ashamed that they can't have the kind of sex life they think they deserve; and/or
- resentful that they're made to feel wrong for their feelings.

All these feelings are valid, and this onslaught of negative emotions are all felt at the same time (by both partners within a few minutes, or even seconds). There's nothing sexy about these feelings. If the higher-desire person views sex as something their partner has the power to give or refuse, then their initiation is going to be laced with the expectation of disappointment, even if it's hidden behind an understanding smile. If the lower-desire person views sex as something their partner uses to just *get off*, then they'll feel used solely for someone else's purposes, and they'll disconnect from their own pleasure.

Understanding what our partner feels and needs and being able to talk honestly about the challenges of initiation without blaming the other party is the first step in healing this unhealthy pattern. Whether we're the higher-desire or lower-desire person in our relationship, sex offers us more than orgasms. We may not even be conscious of the many human needs that lead us to sex – needs like

- physical affection,
- intimate connection,
- being nurtured,
- escape from life's responsibilities,
- erotic excitement,
- sexual validation,
- feeling connected to our bodies below the neck,
- being able to express vulnerability,
- being desired, and
- being accepted for who we are.

We enter relationships hoping to get these needs met yet many couples are stuck in a negative feedback loop of failed initiation and disappointment; the human needs that sex offers go unmet. No matter how hard we try to sweep this "bid and refusal" pattern under the rug, we trip over it in other parts of our relationship. This struggle isn't just felt in moments of initiation: it's an undercurrent that's felt every day, all day.

It sucks!

So I'll share what I tell every couple that comes to me with this "push and pull" dynamic...

Stop!

Stop initiating sex in a way that creates tension repeatedly. Stop reaffirming the negative stories that come up during these moments; stories you tell yourself about your partner and stories you tell yourself about you and your sexuality. Stop disempowering yourself and each other by setting yourselves up for the same experience. Replace the bartering, the hopefulness, and the resistance with something completely different. What that looks like depends on both of you and your willingness to find solutions.

Start talking!

Acknowledge that this dynamic sucks. Confess what it's like for both of you, without blaming the other person. If your current patterns of initiation are leading to tension, get curious about co-creating new approaches to sexual initiation that lead you into each other's arms instead.

35.

The Art of Sexual Initiation (Part 2): Five Elements of a Welcoming Invitation

In the previous chapter, you read about why it's important to master the art of initiation. I use the term "art" because with seduction and initiation there's no formula, no one-size-fits-all script. We learned the importance of understanding our partner's experience and why communication matters. Mastering sexual initiation requires an understanding of desire, attunement, communication, confidence and (yes) disappointment. Let's look next at how these elements play a role in sexual initiation, as a couple.

Start with your own desire

If we're inviting our partner to have sex with us, we want them to feel our authentic desire. If we want our lover to say "yes," we should say "yes" to ourselves first. If we're in touch with our own desire, it shows, and our partner can feel it. Before you approach your partner, take some time to connect to your body: breathe all the way down into your genitals, and start to feel what's going on below the neck. Imagine what it would be like to lie naked next to your lover. Give yourself time to connect to your own desire.

When initiation comes from your own desire, your partner will see it in the softening of your gaze, the deepening of your breath, the feel of your touch, and the sound of your voice. When you connect to your desire, you invite your lover to connect to their own desire. You're not just guiding them into an *activity*: you're guiding them into a *state of receptivity*. You're inviting them into a space of desire and intimacy that you're already occupying, by opening the door and saying, "Come on in, and join me in here."

Attune to your partner and step into confidence

Now that you've connected to your own desire, begin to attune to your partner. Put your phone down, close your laptop, and start to put your attention on them. Offer them some nonsexual touch to guide them out of their heads and into their bodies. Give them time to feel your invitation and connect to their own desire. Sex starts here, with intimate touch and emotional connection. If you're initiating, don't be afraid to take charge. If you're hesitant, nervous about being rejected, or feeling timid (about being seen in your desire), your partner has no lead to follow.

Initiation is where you begin to build sexual polarity and passion. Step up, take the lead, and guide your partner onto the dance floor with confidence. Your partner wants to trust that you have the skill to give them pleasure, and the passion to carry that confident energy throughout your sexual encounter. Confidence comes from within you. Whether you're a woman or a man, initiation requires you to assert yourself and take the risk that you may not get what you want. We all know what it's like to step up in other parts of our lives. Stepping up to initiate sex is no different.

Be direct. Asking for what we want isn't making a demand. It's having the courage to share and show our desire. Being vague, beating around the bush, can come off as wishy-washy. Seduction isn't wishy-washy: it's clear, direct, and confident. Initiation doesn't always have to fall on the shoulders of the dominant partner; the submissive partner can initiate as well. Their invitation may have a different flavor — one that maintains sexual polarity — but their desire can be expressed just as openly and directly. Most dominant partners love to feel desired and pursued by their partner. It's an experience they rarely get and often deeply long for.

Make a date! If spontaneous sex rarely happens, or if you've gotten into a pattern of an emotionally disengaged quickie before sleeping, I encourage couples to plan for sex and give it the attention it deserves. Set a day and time when you both know that you'll have the energy, the privacy, and the *intention* to make sex happen. I know for some, planned sex sounds boring, but what's more boring is ongoing failed attempts to initiate, because of all the excuses we can find to not have sex at any given moment. Make a date with your partner for, say, Saturday at 4:00 PM. Do what you need to do to make it happen. Let that plan percolate for a few days. Enjoy the anticipation. As you move through your week, you both know that Saturday at 4:00 is dedicated to intimacy.

When you both put intimacy on the top of your priority list, you show each other that your relationship matters. When you show up on Saturday afternoon at 4:00, relaxed and ready to be together, you're showing your partner that they matter.

Expand your erotic menu

Once you accept that planned sex may be worth exploring, you have the added option of planning how you're going to spend your upcoming time together.

As an initiator, introduce your partner to the idea of co-creating an "erotic menu." Building erotic menus together opens the door to novelty and variety, the two favorite spices that couples seek. Talk about the energy behind the sexual styles represented in your erotic menu, and what energy you want to bring into your upcoming date. If you're the one to initiate, assure your partner that you're going to take charge of creating the environment to support the energy you want to share, whether that's romantic or kinky. The toys, music, and lighting, for example. all combine to create the mood you both want.

Get good at communicating about sex. If your partner isn't fully on board with your initiation, rather than withdrawing your energy and falling into an internal negative story, get curious. Inquire into what might be holding them back from saying "yes." They might not even know themselves at first, so ask them, "Is there anything that needs to change that would help you say "yes" to spending some intimate time together?"

Reasons to not have sex can range from emotional blocks to practical needs like:

- *I'm too tired, I need to sleep.*
- *I feel full and lethargic after that big meal.*
- *I'm worried about a family member.*
- *I have residual feelings about last night's argument.*
- *The room's not warm enough. The light's too bright.*
- *I feel scattered and distracted.*

All these reasons are valid, and they're all solvable with some communication and action. When we understand that a "no" could just mean, "not under these current conditions" we can help our partner find what they need in order to open themselves to intimacy. Hesitancy and resistance can be misinterpreted as a hard "no." Don't assume your partner is declining your initiation unless it's clearly stated. If their "no" is clearly stated, accept their decision without emotionally disconnecting. If you feel a conversation needs to happen, initiate that instead (when the time is right). If one or both of you suspect that excuses are being used to avoid tougher challenges (like a general lack of desire or a loss of attraction, for example) coaching can help facilitate conversations to move beyond the blocks currently in place.

Navigating disappointment

Learning to handle disappointment when your partner says "no" is perhaps the most important lesson of initiating. I know that may sound self-defeating, but disappointment is going to happen. It's guaranteed! You're in a relationship with another human being who has their own thoughts and feelings. How you handle disappointment is going to set the tone for your entire sexual dynamic. If your pattern is to withdraw, get moody, or lash out, then you're punishing your partner for saying "no." If your partner expects to be emotionally punished for declining your invitation, you're linking sex to a negative experience. Using emotional punishment against your partner only encourages your partner to feel *obliged* to have sex in order to avoid negative emotions.

Obligatory sex is not a turn-on for either partner.

Turn this around by stepping out of the emotional patterns that trigger each other when an initiation is rejected. Cease what's not working and incorporate a more egalitarian approach to sex and intimacy:

- Incorporate planned dates in your life together, and let go of the myth that sex is supposed to just happen spontaneously with the same passion and focus as when you first got together.
- Connect to and show your own desire.
- Attune to your partner, and assess how to support them in getting what they need to be open to intimacy.
- Communicate openly and honestly about both of your desires.
- Find your inner confidence and step into a leadership role.

Disappointments will happen, but stay connected to your partner, even during disappointment, and use good communication skills to move through it together. Remember, sexual initiation in a long-term relationship is not a formula; you and your partner are unique. Your relationship is unique. Honor that!

36.

Sex and Grief:
The Body's Healing Wisdom

Many years ago, a convergence of experiences and losses left me in a state of grief. I cried, I felt sadness, and I rationally accepted life as it was. Yet over the months that followed I felt like I was in a low-grade depression. I spent time with friends and enjoyed day-to-day pleasures, but something inside was not fully moving on.

After a few months I went to see a bodyworker who offered massage in addition to other healing modalities. I didn't share much more with her than my name. She placed her hands on my chest and my lower abdomen and with very little movement started to slowly draw her hand up from my pelvis to my heart. She kept repeating the same slow movement with her hand.

After twenty minutes or so, I could feel something growing in my belly. It was a ball of energy that I sensed traveling up through my chest. When it reached my throat, I let out a loud deep guttural sound that surprised me. Those sounds kept coming until the feeling of the ball of energy inside of me was gone. After a few minutes of feeling calm and relaxed, she continued to draw her hand up to my heart and throat. I could feel the ball of energy again grow in my belly and move slowly up and out of my throat in loud guttural cries. My cries had surprisingly little emotional content, and my breathing was deep and effortless.

My body knew what it was doing.

Cycles like this continued a few more times until, after an hour and a half, there was nothing more, and I felt a deep sense of peace and blissful emptiness. My body had released my unprocessed grief. No one had to tell me that; I could feel it.

Before I left, I shared my experience with the bodyworker. I told her it was similar to feeling an orgasm slowly building in my pelvic region, but rather than it moving down and out through the genitals, the energy moved up and out of my throat. My body knew what to do. All I had to do was focus my attention, continue breathing deeply, and marvel at my body's inherent wisdom and healing power.

Love, reality & grief

Years later I delivered a talk to a group of cancer survivors in a local hospital. We were talking about how to use sex to help heal from the grief that comes with illness. Each woman shared her journey with cancer, each expressing how welcoming touch and pleasure again became an important part of their healing. I came away from that talk feeling even more deeply that sex is a healer, and when the time is right, orgasmic energy can play an important part in connecting us to our bodies and experiencing feelings of all kinds, not just the sexy ones!

There's much to feel these days. If we slow down enough to feel it, grief surrounds us. Untimely deaths, environmental degradation, relationship breakups, unwanted change, aging... we're all grieving, both personally and globally. Grief has taken a seat at all our tables.

So where does sex fit into grief? The myth is that these two very basic human experiences are mutually exclusive. We believe we shouldn't want sex until we're feeling sexy and receptive, and we can't be grieving if our bodies are turned-on and orgasmic. But this isn't necessarily so. Everyone needs to honor their own journey through grief. Grief is not something to be measured by time. It presents itself differently for every person, but is it possible to allow grief to be part of our sexual experience?

Grief is an isolating experience. We become lost in our own subjective pain, and even find refuge in our retreat from society; but after some time, the need for isolation is replaced with the need for connection. When the time comes to reach out and take the hand of a caring lover, a new phase of healing begins. We can open the door and let them into our private pain.

Intimacy takes on an even deeper meaning. When we let ourselves be seen in our most vulnerable and raw states, we can allow ourselves to be held and touched, and receive all the hormonal and mental benefits that touch brings. By seeing ourselves through the loving eyes of another, our pain is shared, and our burden is eased.

Pleasure never leaves us; we leave pleasure. Even when we move through difficult emotions, pleasure is always there; like a bridge over troubled water, pleasure can reconnect us to our bodies. By focusing on arousal, physical pleasure drags us out of our subjective thoughts and into the present moment. The present moment is free of the past and the future, both of which weigh heavily on us during times of grief. Letting go into pleasure, feeling the buildup of orgasmic energy, and trusting that it's okay to let pleasure move in us, can help shift us out of the *deep freeze* of loss.

With the use of deep breath and arousal, energy gets unstuck and our emotional armor relaxes. If you've ever cried during sex, you know that tears and orgasm are strangely similar in their release. They both move energy through our bodies in a way that's physically healthy and emotionally healing.

Lovers in a dangerous time

It's wonderful to feel the love of others in trying times, but the real power of love during grief is the *giving* of love, as much as the *getting*. We can become absorbed in grief and loss. That's part of the grieving process as well, but when the time is right, we can turn our gaze from inward pain and outward to our beloved standing by us, ready to help.

Sending loving energy shifts us out of our left brain — where fight, flight, and freeze operate — into the part of our right brain that houses things like gratitude, empathy, and compassion. The act of *giving love* is like placing a healing salve on a wounded brain. It gives our exhausted, high-alert mind a place to rest and be nourished.

Anyone who meditates will tell you about the clarity and emotional transcendence that comes from focused attention. Stop reading right now and place your thumb and finger together. Move them so slowly and with so much attention that you can feel the ridges of your fingerprints. Do this for a few breaths and see how long you can give your full attention to this experience. You've just momentarily cleared your mind of its outward thinking!

Sexual pleasure draws us into our bodies and for a while puts the rest of the world on hold. Sex and orgasm offer an escape from our overly active minds. In letting go and allowing an orgasm to happen, we take a momentary leave from the weightiness of our world. In addition to clearing our minds, orgasms also move stuck energy in our bodies.

If we're carrying grief, orgasmic energy can move through us with a healing force.

You don't see grief or sad feelings in porn. You rarely see sex and grief in films or TV. Sex is usually depicted as a one-note emotional experience of passion or romance. If your partner is experiencing grief, here are some things to remember when it comes to sex and intimacy:

- Offer nonsexual touch and affection without expectations of anything more. Allow your partner to find their way back to sex in their own time. If they want to be sexual, keep the *sexy* out of it, and assure them that they don't have to feel anything other than what they're feeling (which is probably not very sexy).

- Having sex during sadness or grief is a multi-emotional experience. Emotions flow and intermingle. Tears can change into laughter and vice versa. Your partner may feel alive one moment and numb the next. The grieving partner needs to flow with whatever arises without judgment. Joining in sex with a grieving partner requires us to stay attuned to whatever feeling is present, and whatever our partner needs in that moment.

- Encourage them to breathe fully and relax into the pleasure of physical contact without any pressure to perform or reciprocate.

- Create a slow, relaxed pace so they have the time to connect to their pleasure and become aroused in their own time. Allow arousal to build slowly and gently.

- Be prepared for loss of erections or lack of lubrication. Our bodies know what they want. If intercourse is off the table, turn your attention to whatever feels pleasurable to your partner. Help them ask for what they want and follow their lead.

There is no *place* to get to. This kind of lovemaking can be relaxed and meandering. Orgasms may or may not happen. Leave your agenda at the bedroom door. Incorporate breaks to share your thoughts, if needed, or simply stay silent while holding or cradling. Tears may flow. Stay in connection and encourage them to feel what they're feeling. Be a rock when they feel unstable and let them know you've got them.

37.

Tell Me What You Want:
Looking Inside Americas' Erotic Mind

Did you know that the most common sexual fantasies for Republicans are infidelity and orgies, while Democrats most enjoy BDSM fantasies?

I've been enjoying Kinsey Research Fellow Justin Lehmiller's book *Tell Me What You Want: The Science of Sexual Desire and How It Can Help You Improve Your Sex Life*. I'm enjoying it probably because I agree with most of what he says. (Funny how that works.) Aren't we *all* curious about what other people think and do when it comes to sex?

Lehmiller's book is chock full of statistics that come from the largest survey ever undertaken of Americans' sexual fantasies. Over a two-year period, 4,000 people answered 350 questions about sex and fantasy.

The biggest finding? *Fantasizing about sex is normal*.

- 97% have sexual fantasies, and most reported having them frequently;
- 89% said that multiple partner sex is a common favorite;
- 60% said that fantasies about sadomasochism, or playing with erotic pain, turns them on;

- 51% prefer their current partner to be the star in their fantasy; and
- Less than one third said they had acted out their biggest fantasy.

Lehmiller shares the sexual fantasies of our fellow humans in detail; in so doing, he helps to normalize the sexual fantasies with which we're all walking around yet trying to hide. We must ask: If we're all fantasizing, why do so many people suffer from low sexual desire?

Low sex drive is one of the more common complaints I hear from couples in my coaching practice. For what *kind* of sex do they have a low drive? Is it the kind of sex we're told we *should* be having? Or the kind of sex we actually *want*? Such questions reveal most sexual challenges are far more psychological than physiological.

This is not news in the world of sex therapy. It wasn't until the 1960s that sex researchers Masters and Johnson shared what they learned from studying hundreds of couples. They discovered that communication and intimacy are the path to sexual desire.

Why are communication and intimacy so important? When we talk to our partner about something as intimate as sexual fantasies and sexual desires, we reveal our sexual selves, which in turn leads to deeper intimacy and trust. By sharing our erotic fantasies, we're saying, "I feel safe enough with you to share this part of myself."

Your desires are beautiful

I have a client who confessed that she never has sexual fantasies! This fact in and of itself brought up feelings of shame. We talked about where her mind goes if she knows she's going to have sex with her partner. She realized her fantasies weren't about hot sex as much as they were about having the perfect date night where she feels deeply loved and desired. She did in fact have a fantasy life, one that worked for her to elicit feelings of anticipation and excitement.

As Lehmiller's survey findings show us, that we all have fantasies, and many of them are common themes and scenarios. Fantasies range from mild to wild. They can be highly visual or more feeling based. Many of them are common themes and others are more unusual. With 97 percent of us admitting we have sexual fantasies, we can confidently say it's *normal*. Knowing we're all normal helps us to accept our imaginings, which is the first step in finding peace with our sexual selves. It's also the first step in finding the confidence to share our fantasies with our partners.

Although I've written about sexual fantasies before, I want to explain why many couples find themselves struggling with low desire, orgasm challenges, and erection issues. I agree with Lehmiller that in many cases the answer lies in *sexual repression*. We're not born sexually repressed. As most parents will agree, babies and young children are very open about their bodies and what gives them pleasure. We learn sexual repression from the world around us. We're indoctrinated into believing that sex is wrong or shameful and therefore not something to be discussed openly.

If almost all of us have sexual thoughts and fantasies but we believe deep down that it's wrong to talk about sex, then we'll repress our thoughts and hide our true selves from the person with whom we're intimate. When we repress our authentic sexuality — out of shame or fear — it shows up in our ability to be vulnerable, to let ourselves go, to feel confident, and to be shame-free in our sex lives. The key to being able to share our fantasies and desires is the belief that our partner's response will be positive and accepting. The survey participants who said they don't share their fantasies said it was from fear of their partner's judgment.

In my online course, *Your Erotic Menu*, I coach couples on how to talk about sex openly and (most importantly) how to share in a way that feels safe and exciting. I encourage partners to hear each other's fantasies without judgment, and to say in response, "Your desires are beautiful."

The safer we make it for our partners to share openly, the deeper will be the intimacy and trust.

Here's a fact to keep in mind: the vast majority of the survey participants who shared their favorite fantasy with their partner said their partner's response was either favorable or (at least) neutral. I hope this gives you some confidence to take the leap and let your partner access your erotic mind.

Research shows that couples who are comfortable sharing their sexual fantasies

- feel more love towards each other;
- have less problematic sex lives;
- have fewer challenges around erections and orgasms;
- are more attracted to the person they self-disclosed to; and
- experience higher sexual self-confidence.

Sharing our sexual selves doesn't come without risk, but the risk of revealing who we are to our partner offers the far greater reward of building trust and intimacy.

38.

Lay Your Heart on the Table:
Ten Tips for Sharing Your Sexual Desires

Sex is probably one of the hardest things to discuss with a partner. It's easy to take things personally because sex is deeply personal. Confessing our desires and asking for what we want takes courage and trust that your partner will hold your feelings with care. If sex is difficult for you to discuss, the best thing to do is to start talking but do it in a way that you both feel heard and understood.

Put aside time for a private conversation. Wait until you both feel relaxed and your minds are clear (from work, kids, chores, unresolved disagreements, and the other concerns of daily life). Turn off your phones. (Seriously!) Get cozy and make physical contact. Set the scene to explore feelings and be ready to listen deeply. This isn't about trying to get someone to behave as you wish; it's about confessing *your* desires and listening to *theirs*! Don't wait until you're exhausted at the end of the day: carve out moments for conversation when you have the energy to talk and listen. Many of my clients are self-conscious about closing their bedroom door during the day for alone time if they have family in the house. Show your family members that you prioritize and value your relationship by taking time to nurture it, whether it's for talking, cuddling, or sex. That's good modeling!

Take turns. It never works when two people try to share at the same time. If one of you is sharing, the other needs to only listen until they're finished talking. Stay open-hearted and open-minded without words or looks of judgment and shaming. Don't interrupt! Be patient until they've said what they want to say. When they're finished, you can ask if there's anything else they'd like to add. And then *thank them for sharing*. Ask them how they felt about sharing their desires. They might have felt nervous about it and now feel relieved. Or they might suddenly feel embarrassed or afraid of being rejected. Be sensitive to their feelings and remember that our erotic minds are all unique! We can't fully understand where our desires come from, but we can listen with an open and curious heart.

Ask open-ended questions and get curious about your partner. Many people have trouble asking for what they want sexually. Some don't honestly believe they *deserve* to get what they want, so be a receptive listener. Right now, this is about them, not you. When you've had time for some questions and answers, notice your feelings:

- Do you feel threatened that your sexual tastes might be different?
- Are you feeling pressured to do something you don't want to do?
- Do you feel insecure that your partner might not want you if you don't share the same desires?
- Can you communicate difficult feelings without blaming them for making you feel that way?
- Do you feel touched that your partner has spoken their truth and demonstrated their trust in you to hear it.

Think of conversations about sex as a newborn baby: Protect it from harm, hold it tenderly, and nurture it with loving attention. Take turns sharing your desires, knowing your partner is holding space for you to open up. If difficult feelings arise, stay with them. This is where you can both practice your communication skills. If one of you is triggered, listen to their fears with empathy. Sometimes that's all it takes for those fears to subside. It's a process of learning and accepting one another that doesn't happen overnight. Trust is built by consistent, small gestures, not grand promises! Even if our partner's chosen activity isn't our cup of tea, be curious about what it is that turns them on. Listen to their thoughts and insights and be open to the possibility that you might discover your *own* turn-on while trying something new!

If one person prefers an evening of romance and tender lovemaking, make a date to fill their cup with exactly what they desire, down to the details. If the other wants to get tied up and objectified, plan a time to give them that experience, so they get their cup filled as well! When you give your partner an experience you know they love that's not "your thing," draw from the sheer pleasure of enjoying their turn-on, knowing you're giving them what they want with a generous and loving heart. Trust that they'll do the same for you when the time is right.

Your primary sexual needs might not align perfectly but you could find yourselves expanding your sexual menus to include a variety of experiences. Think about it: If your partner was your sexual clone, your sex life would lack the erotic tension that comes with difference!

Keep the words flowing. Our words let others into our heart. Bring an open-hearted curiosity to each other's erotic minds. Judgment closes the door to learning and erodes trust. A roll of the eyes, a snide comment, a joke, a look of disapproval, silence — all have the power to close down the subject, to never be brought up again. Remember, your partner is no more responsible for their erotic turn-ons than they are the color of their eyes. Rather than seeing them as a problem, learn how differences broaden the playing field. Celebrate a full spectrum of love!

Make these conversations part of your life together. If we begin sensitive conversations by reassuring our partner that they're loved and respected, curiosity and interest will take the place of fear. Be courageous enough to lay your heart on the table and start talking!

39.

You Can't Argue Someone into Loving You: An Open Letter to Higher-Desire Partners Who Are Pissed

You can't argue someone into loving you, yet in effect that's the conflict in which many *no-sex* or *low-sex* couples find themselves. Chronic anger around a couple's sexuality poisons a relationship and stresses their emotional bond. When the higher-desire partner badgers, guilt trips, nags, pouts, barters or begs for sex, they unwittingly turn sex into a commodity to be acquired, an argument to be won. While such pressure tactics can work outside of the bedroom, power struggles in the bedroom only end in frustration and conflict. It sounds obvious, but couples in long-term relationships continuously get trapped in this destructive dynamic.

This clearly self-defeating dynamic doesn't happen overnight: it develops over time as a toxic response to a seemingly unsolvable sexual standoff. This standoff places trusted partners at odds with each other, setting them up as combatants fighting for their position and perspective while under the pressure of conflict and disconnection. It's a lose/lose strategy that leads either to separation or resignation that neither partner will enjoy their desired sex life. The higher-desire partner feels like they have no choice but to push through the lower-desire partner's resistance in order to convert them to the idea they should have sex. The request for sex is often laced with anxiety; if there's a history of refusal, resentment will lurk under the surface. This is not a winning strategy for intimacy of any kind.

Please understand: I don't want to minimize the hurt and disappointment of the higher-desire partner. It's not easy to be continuously rejected when we make ourselves vulnerable enough to ask for sex and affection. At some point, the higher-desire partner may choose to stop initiating altogether, to avoid the pain of rejection. Ongoing rejection creates all sorts of negative thoughts and beliefs:

- *I'm unattractive.*
- *I'm a bad lover.*
- *I'll never get what I want and need.*
- *I'm being punished.*
- *The future of my relationship is uncertain.*

All these negative thoughts lead to an underlying stress that permeates the relationship and undermines trust and intimacy – the very things necessary for desire to be present. Both partners suffer greatly in this power struggle. Even when sex does happen, the undercurrent of resentment of both parties can make sex feel mechanical and emotionally guarded. Is it surprising then that one or both partners lose interest in sex altogether? Being argued into having sex is like being pressured into giving someone your car keys or loaning them a treasured book. Sex is not a thing to borrow or a favor you perform for your partner to appease their anger and ease tension. Sex is a mutual experience — a *space* you both agree to enter into together for intimacy and fulfillment. The only way to gain an enthusiastic "yes" to sex is to attract your partner into entering that intimate space with you. Unlike coercion, attraction takes thought, investigation, curiosity, and creativity.

I remember, years ago, the words of a male client, who suddenly stood up from his chair and proclaimed:

"I married my partner with the understanding that sex would be an important part of our marriage," he proclaimed. "I didn't change my mind about that. She did. I have a right to be angry, and I've told her that!"

I agreed with his sentiments and his emotions: he had every right to feel like he'd lost something important to him. Yet it was also clear he wasn't going to find what he was looking for via anger or guilt-tripping his wife. When I asked what he liked most about sex with his wife, he softened. He started speaking about the closeness they once shared in intimate moments. He missed the touching and the connection. He spoke about the feeling of escaping the outside world together for a while.

"I miss her," he finally said, like it was a sudden insight. "If I can't share that kind of experience with her anymore then I'm just living with a roommate. It's not what I want, and I don't think it's what she wants either."

His anger melted into sadness and disappointment.

"Have you told her lately what you love about having sex with her?" I asked him. "Have you *ever* told her that you miss her?

"This is what she needs to hear," I added. "Not that she's wrong for losing interest in sex, or that she should have sex whether she wants to or not."

If you wanted your partner to swim across a pond to join you on the other side, you wouldn't throw a rock at them to pressure them into crossing; you'd more likely toss them a life jacket to make their trip across easier. In this scenario, intimacy or connection is the lifejacket you toss over. Note also that attracting our partner into intimacy requires us to first become intimate ourselves — to become vulnerable and honest about the unexpressed feelings we harbor underneath the anger or coercion. When we approach our partner with our offensive armor down, they'll feel safe to lower their defenses. We can ask for a truce in the daily sexual power struggle so that honest words can be spoken without blame or judgment.

We're all responsible for our circumstances; the roles of *victim* and *perpetrator* don't have a place in my sessions. There are no purely innocent parties. Once this dynamic is understood and released, healing and a new dynamic can take its place. Here are some initial steps to consider:

Talk about it. This is easier said than done, I know. If conversations about sex are charged with blame and defensiveness, then you're going to have to wipe that slate clean and come into the conversation with your *white flags* up. Let your partner know you want to work on your sexuality as a *team* and end the pattern of conflict around sex.

Take responsibility. Own your part in creating the push-pull dynamic around sex. If you have challenges controlling your anger or criticism, find a coach who can teach you some tools to use when you're triggered. It will change your life!

Speak from your experience. Offer your partner vulnerability and share your disappointment rather than your judgment.

Be curious. Investigate your partner's relationship to sex and how they feel about your sex life together. If they feel safe from emotional punishment they'll open up about their needs and desires.

Ask questions. With sincere interest, help your partner share their deepest truth. There are many reasons behind sexual inhibition or reluctance (too many to list here).

Be patient. If you don't get the hoped-for open-hearted response the first time, stay the course. Entrenched patterns take time to shift. Trust takes time to build. Let them experience the change *in you* first so they can find their own change in response.

Seek help. Finally, and most importantly, know that you don't have to go it alone! Your journey back to fulfilling, intimate, erotic sex could benefit from the help of a professional. Think of it as the difference between a dangerous slog through the jungle and a fun, safe, guided safari adventure.

To paraphrase the Bard:

All the bedroom's a stage, and all the men and women merely players; they have their fears and their strategies, and one person in their time plays many parts...

40.

Desire Discrepancy:
The Plight of the Lower-Desire Partner

Sexual desire *discrepancy* in long-term relationships isn't an anomaly; it's built into the lifestyle of cohabitation and is pretty much guaranteed to develop at some point within the first couple of years in a new relationship. Desire discrepancy is normal and to be expected, yet it remains one of the most painful and destabilizing challenges a couple must face. This dynamic pits partners against each other in a battle of blame, guilt, and defensiveness. Given the reluctance most couples have to talk about sex openly, it's hardly surprising that differences in sexual desire become a cauldron of mistaken presumptions, misunderstandings, and unspoken shame. The higher-desire partner feels shame about their role as sole initiator, and the lower-desire partner feels shame about their lack of desire for sex. Both become stuck in their story of *failing at sex*. They've lost the safety and security they once had in the sanctuary of each other's arms.

Nature giveth and nature taketh away

New relationships are fueled by novelty and sexual intensity. Nature sets us up for procreation by pumping us with feel-good hormones like serotonin and norepinephrine. When sex is infused with the natural high of these hormones, it can lead to unrealistic expectations that the relationship will continue forever with this kind of intensity and mutual desire. Gazing at each other through rose-colored glasses, we tell ourselves we've finally found our perfect sexual match.

After one to three years in a relationship, the infatuation hormones slowly fade. Sexual desires shift, sexual frequency changes, and the higher-desire partner is left to wonder what happened to their sweetheart's ready and willing state of arousal. The lower-desire partner becomes mired in feelings of guilt and defensiveness. Add in the sometimes daily pressure for sex from their partner and sex becomes a quagmire of negative emotions that kills desire and builds resistance.

This initial phase of disillusionment is the time when couples need to start talking about sex in an open and honest way. Rather than accusing our partner of changing or viewing each other as adversaries with competing needs, couples can pull together and view themselves as a *sexual team*, equally responsible for their sex life's health and wellness. This is where their work begins as a *sexually engaged couple*.

We can thank books, movies, and (especially) porn for perpetuating the great lie. What is this lie? That sex is always hot, spontaneous, and satisfying for both parties; that sex always includes strong, long-lasting erections, ever-ready lubricated vaginas, and endings with mutually coinciding orgasms. As most long-term couples will tell you, this isn't the case. Sex is more varied than what we're fed by the media. Real sex isn't a "performance" that goes from zero to sixty in less than a minute. Real sex is more relaxed: it's authentic, sometimes awkward, sometimes messy, and all of this makes real sex more vulnerable than anything you see on a screen. It's not performed to "entertain" or hold the undivided attention of anyone watching. (*Well, not usually...*)

Statistics tell a more accurate story. Roughly 40 to 50 percent of sexual encounters in long-term relationships are mutually satisfying; 25 percent are better for one partner than the other; and 15 percent will be unsatisfying for both. Knowing this and having realistic expectations allows couples to relax when they don't quite hit their "high bar." If your relationship is nurtured with regular *nonsexual* affection and loving gestures outside of the bedroom, you'll feel more relaxed when sex occasionally falls short. Couples with a healthy openness in their sex life can let it go — even laugh it off — and accept that sex isn't always going to meet the mark. And that's okay!

The plight of the lower-desire partner

Unlike the higher-desire partner, whose focus is sex, the lower-desire partner has to contend with *resistance*. Resistance isn't always easy to understand, even when it's our own. As you know by now from reading this book, discussing sexuality, sensuality, and intimacy is key. Shame-filled silence will keep us hidden in our self-doubt and self-judgment.

If the lower-desire partner assumes the burden is on them alone to figure it out, guilt, shame, and resentment will drive underground any potential for desire. When we approach sex as a team, the challenge around desire is shared by both partners. When sex is blame and guilt-free we feel open to exploring solutions that meet both partners' needs.

It's helpful to understand that desire presents itself differently to different people. Higher-desire partners may experience desire in a more spontaneous way – with the experience of sex *descending* upon them. They might start to feel aroused physically, or sexual desire will infiltrate their thoughts out of the blue; they could find themselves lost in a sexual fantasy. Desire will present itself, and they'll feel moved to have sex. It's natural for them to assume desire moves in everyone like this.

Higher-desire partners wonder if their partner even desires them since they never initiate sex.

Lower-desire partners might experience desire quite differently, for instance as a response to stimuli that arouses them. If you were to ask them if they're interested in having sex, their response might initially be "no." But once they open themselves to arousing stimuli — whether in the form of touch, visuals, or seductive words — and if the invitation is made in a way that attracts them, then responsive desire starts to move in them. These are the people who will admit to not wanting sex initially but to enjoying the sex once things get rolling.

Owning your turn-ons and turnoffs

If resistance plays a role in your sexuality, it's time to investigate. Sit down and write a list of the things that turn you on — and the things that turn you off — to the idea of having sex. Often *conditions* play a big role in our "yes" and "no." You might be surprised to see what's on your list of turn-ons. Examples include

- having transition time between work and play;
- knowing the kids are out of the house and won't knock on the door;
- feeling energized after a run;
- listening to certain music;
- dancing and being silly together; and
- reading an erotic story;

Your turnoffs might include:

- having sex after a big meal when you're feeling full and tired;
- jumping into sex without first emotionally connecting with your partner;

- feeling too rushed to find your own pleasure;
- the lights being too bright, the room being too cold; or
- worrying that your body won't perform as you wish.

Make a list of five to ten of your own *openers* and *closers*, so you can see them all on paper, and share it with your partner. They'll better understand how desire works for you so they can support the conditions that help you open up.

Breaking the habit of resistance

Resistance is sneaky. It'll show up even before you've given sex much thought. It may whispermessages based on fears and insecurities:

- *My partner doesn't find me attractive anymore.*
- *I take too long to orgasm.*
- *I'm a boring lover.*
- *My kids will walk in on us.*
- *I'm afraid to ask for a certain sexual experience.*
- *I'll lose my erection.*
- *I'll never meet my partner's needs.*
- *I need to drink or get high before sex.*
- *I fear painful or dysfunctional sex and can't do anything about it.*
- *I dislike the pressure of being someone I'm not during sex.*

Start to observe the thoughts behind your resistance and question if they're true or not. Talk to your partner about the negative beliefs that contribute to your resistance. If you're working as a sexual team, your partner will appreciate your sharing. Ask them to help you rewrite your negative thoughts into positive affirmations that feed your self-confidence and self-esteem.

Saying No with Love

Saying "no" to our partner's initiation is hard on both people. "No" is a door closer and leaves little room for any other thoughts or solutions. If you're usually a "no" to sexual intercourse, as a pattern, ask yourself what you might be a "yes" to? Get curious about what you're open to and learn how to deliver your "no" in a way that doesn't slam the door in your partner's face. Couch your "no" with a statement of appreciation like, "I'm too tired to have intercourse right now, but I appreciate your desire to be close. Would you like to have an orgasm another way?" Or "I'm looking forward to being sexual with you. Can we set a date for tomorrow rather than tonight?" Before you answer your partner's request for sex with a defensive "no," feel your partner's own vulnerability in their request and ask for what you want from a place of connection. Coming together as a sexually empowered team will keep sex alive and well, *for real*.

41.

Ethical Porn:
Beyond the Mainstream

Watching other people have sex is tucked deep into our DNA. We're drawn to it out of curiosity, the thrill of voyeurism, the excitement of arousal, and the all-time big driver in our human bodies: the desire to procreate. Watching others have sex has signaled the desire to have sex ourselves since time immemorial. As a sex and relationship coach, I see how porn tends to pit partners against each other and can lead a couple down the road of sexual shame, secrecy, and mistrust.

It doesn't have to be this way.

I'd like to widen your definition of porn and share some thoughts on how it can be used as a tool for sexual communication and exploration. Whether you defend porn or deplore it, you'll find heaps of opinions that support you and large swaths of people who will vehemently disagree with you. Porn is not an argument to be won, or even a problem to be solved; pornography or *erotica* is something to be discussed, understood, and (for those who are inclined) integrated into a relationship as a tool to enhance your sex life rather than damage it.

Pornography (depictions of people having sex for the purpose of arousing the viewer) has been around for hundreds or even thousands of years. The internet has made porn so ubiquitous in our society that, these days, pretty much everyone has seen porn of some kind, and most of us have formed our position for or against it based on our sexual identities, our views on freedom of speech, our moral judgments, and our human rights perspectives.

It's hard to pigeonhole porn these days. Like everything else, porn is changing and expanding. Whether it was yesteryear's 8mm "stag films" or the more sophisticated Betamax or VHS videos of the 1980s that interspersed sex scenes with campy plots, the multi-billion-dollar porn industry evolved from the perspective of cameramen and businessmen creating increasingly explicit content for a primarily male consumer audience. The industry has more recently tilted toward decentralization, which has resulted in better conditions for actors and less abuse. A more direct and personalized experience is emerging via platforms like LiveCam, and OnlyFans sites that, in effect, make it possible to earn money from broadcasting erotic experiences directly from a person's bedroom to paying customers. With the evolution of technology like VR headsets, porn will survive and thrive in forms we can barely imagine. And with blockchain technology, it will be difficult if not impossible to ban or censor.

Even within the latest censorship laws (in the United States these are known as "FOSTA-SESTA") that make it nearly impossible to use the word "sex" anymore in social media platforms (including the words "sex education"!), porn will, I have no doubt, remain one of the most sought-after subjects on the internet. When a society suppresses sexuality in the form of porn, it's probably also suppressing healthy sex education, as we see in schools across the country. Without an open, shame-free forum for sex education, we're left with the lies and stereotypes that mainstream porn imparts. This shows up in sexual challenges for our young people today.

Click Here Now!

Mainstream porn entertainment is designed to entice you into watching more of it. If porn was based on real-life sex, we'd likely become bored watching it. Why? Because real sex often includes things like seduction, touching, and relaxed orgasmic build-up. Sometimes it includes awkwardness, or messiness. Sometimes it's amazing, and sometimes it falls a little short. That's the way *real* sex is. The delicious nuances that make for great sex can't be experienced from the outside. These unseen factors are felt between the people engaged in intimacy, including connection, presence, chemistry, and vulnerability. This isn't exactly *clickbait material* for the ever-decreasing human attention span that's now approaching that of a *goldfish* (so they say).

We need to differentiate between mainstream porn — which makes money from clicks and ads, imparts misinformation, sets us up for impossible expectations, and desensitizes us to reality — and porn that's potentially useful as a tool to help couples discover and enjoy their erotic desires. One of the more common complaints I hear from couples about porn is that one partner watches it privately, while the other feels betrayed and becomes judgmental.

Understandably, secrecy born out of fear of judgment doesn't lend itself to a happy, secure relationship. Whether it's porn or online shopping, if we believe the only way to avoid conflict is to go underground, then it's time for some honest conversations and agreements! "Coming out of the porn closet" might seem scary, but surprising conversations can take place given the right environment. Porn use is just one of many topics of conversation in my sex and intimacy coaching. If there's tension between partners about porn, these conversations may hurt a little at first, but the healing that comes with honest sharing is well worth the initial discomfort.

The reasons behind watching porn are varied and depend on the circumstances. People turn to porn for all sorts of reasons — including stress release, curiosity, novelty, and exploration of desires — as well as current dissatisfaction with sex. If viewing porn is having a negative impact on a relationship, both partners need to sit down and really listen to each other (maybe for the first time). Some couples have never spoken about porn without inflicting shame, blame, and judgment on each other. Take away the emotional battering and a conversation about porn can lead to all sorts of shared insights and perspectives. There's far more to porn these days than the aforementioned mainstream, male-focused fare that's so easy and free to find.

I'd like to point out the ways in which porn, in its most ethical forms, can help couples tune in and turn on to online sex. Since porn is here to stay, let's look at what's out there, and how to discern between the good, the bad, and the ugly!

Ethical porn in a (largely) unethical industry

This is what Google says about ethical porn:

> Ethical porn can be defined as that which is made legally, respects the rights of performers, has good working conditions, shows both fantasy and real-world sex and celebrates sexual diversity.

You're more likely to find "ethical porn" when you move from the larger mainstream porn sites to paid or subscription sites that are independently produced and distributed. These smaller productions companies make more diverse content showing a wider range of body types, genders, races, and different sexual activities. Most importantly, it includes a woman's perspective (in front of the camera and behind it); since one-in-four people who watch porn are women, this is a game changer! If we only expose ourselves to the same types of people and a limited depiction of what sex looks like, we're going to severely narrow our own expectations with a real partner and come to believe that sex only looks a certain way.

Ethical porn doesn't support harmful racial and gender stereotypes. It often shows consent conversations on screen and underlines the importance of pleasure for all involved. Off screen, the working conditions are safe, and the wages are fair. In other words, the actors have *agency* and are treated *respectfully*.

Watching ethically produced productions removes the dissonance that arises around all the injustices commonly found in mainstream porn. Most women I work with do not want to see the misogyny and stereotypes that a lot of male-focused porn promotes; because these women know very little about alternatives to the mainstream fare, they understandably refuse to watch porn at all. They end up judging their partner's porn viewing habits by this metric, which tends to drive their partner's porn-watching underground. The breach of trust, along with the disapproval of porn as they know it, will shut down further conversations about porn, leaving both partners feeling misunderstood.

Asking our reluctant partner to explore new styles of porn that might appeal to them is a conversation that requires sensitivity and tact! Do your homework first and give your partner links to sites geared to their sexual style, whether that's romantic and sensual or wild and kinky. Let them do their own research without you looking over their shoulder. Ask them to choose one or two sites that engage their imagination and share them with you when you have some private time together. Assure them that your interest in watching porn together is about enhancing your sex life together, not replacing them with fantasies about porn stars. Talk about the reasons why couples enjoy watching porn together, and (of course) read this chapter together.

Watching ethical porn together

Let's explore the reasons some couples might want to watch ethically-produced porn together. One reason might be a *lack of sexual experience*. When a person hasn't had many sexual partners, they're curious about sex. What's normal? How do other couples have sex? What does pleasure look like with other couples? By imagining themselves in the roles of the actors, individuals and couples can start to enjoy watching their fantasies played out by others before exploring new experiences themselves. If the porn is realistic, it gives them confidence to step into new forms of sexual expression.

Amateur porn introduces us to sex-positive couples who like to make their *own porn* for others to watch. By example, they teach us that sex doesn't have to be shameful and hidden. We can empower our relationship to sex by watching others express and share what turns them on.

Couples can find novel ideas to expand their erotic menu. Many people will admit they still have sex the same way they did in high school. Yet our sexuality can change like any other part of our life. When we watch porn together, we expose ourselves to new sexual styles and energies and evolve (both in terms of how we see ourselves, and how our partner sees us). Partners can find sexual acts or activities that excite them and then share them with their partner. Kicking off a conversation about things you find exciting isn't always easy. By doing some solo investigation, we can find porn that turns us on, and share our desires with our partner.

We can also learn about our partner's erotic fantasy life and distinguish between things they want to try and things they'd prefer just to fantasize about. Liking a certain kind of porn doesn't mean you *have to*, or even *want to*, experience it for real.

Diversity in porn includes age. Porn focuses predominantly on younger people, giving the message that older folks either don't watch porn, want to see younger bodies, or don't care about sex that much anymore, none of which is necessarily true (at all!) Many years ago, during my own sexual education I watched porn featuring a couple in their seventies. I was touched by the mood and energy of their lovemaking. They looked extremely relaxed with their bodies, and their relationship to their sexuality was confident and emotionally connected. They laughed, talked during sex, and enjoyed post-orgasm intimacy in each other's arms. It depicted sex as a lifetime enjoyment that has no age limit. Now that I'm one of the older folks myself, I coach many seniors in having fulfilling sex lives.

It's easy to get drawn into porn rabbit holes that aren't necessarily your bag and shut you down to looking any further. If you want to explore ethical online porn, here are a few resources to point you in the right direction:

1. Watch a TED Talk given by Cindy Gallop (www.makelovenotporn.tv):
    https://www.ted.com/talks/cindy_gallop_make_love_not_porn

2. Read an article on Erika Lust, just one of many female porn directors who are changing the face of porn:
    https://www.harpersbazaar.com/culture/features/a20471/how-female-filmmakers-are-reinventing-porn-for-stylish-women/

3. Read an article about a senior couple who agreed to star in an Erika Lust film:
    https://melmagazine.com/en-us/story/why-these-seniors-decided-to-start-making-porn-in-their-seventies

4. Learn about the world of erotica and the power of the written word. You don't have to sit in front of a screen to get turned on! **https://www.frolicme.com**

5. Check out *Dipsea*. It's an app that is focused on helping women tap into their sexuality more easily through the power of storytelling. Listening to erotica can be a great way to close your eyes and allow your multitasking brain to take a break. **https://www.dipseastories.com**

I hope this opens your eyes to the fact that there's a wide variety of porn available for those who dislike the mainstream commercialized variety. Spend a bit of money and support porn and erotica that promote inclusivity, authenticity, and sex positivity for all genders and sexual styles!

42.

Welcome To My Mind:
Sharing Fantasies with Your Partner

I spoke with one client about her discomfort with talking about her fantasies and sex in general. I asked her to tell me about one of her favorite past lovers and the way she felt when she was with him.

"He was adventurous and was very open about sex," she answered. "I didn't have any shame or shyness when I was with him. He encouraged me to share my most exciting fantasies with him."

"Having a conversation about fantasies was extremely liberating for me," she continued, "and we used fantasy during sex to turn each other on. It felt playful and creative. I told him that I've always fantasized about having a threesome with another woman. I'd never shared that with anyone before."

We never actually had a threesome," she said, "but talking about it, and even planning it at one point, was really exciting in and of itself."

This woman had the experience of being with someone who opened her up. He led by example, and in so doing gave her permission to overcome her shyness and share her threesome fantasy. He helped her connect to a part of herself that felt free and willing to take some risks in revealing herself.

Who we are sexually is often influenced by the partner we're with. We affect each other's level of sexual freedom and authenticity. In order to support one another's sexual growth and learning, ask your partner if they'd be interested in sharing their sexual fantasies for the purpose of deepening your sexual connection and expanding your erotic experience. When we're tuned into our partner's erotic mind, we can support them having the experience to which they're drawn. Sharing our erotic fantasies with our partner is the 2.0 level of sexual communication.

Take the leap

Letting our partner into our erotic mind is scary. We trust that they won't shame us, judge us, or (bottom line) stop loving us. It feels risky. Maybe you're worried that they'll share your sexual fantasies with their friends, or worse, use this very personal information against you in some way during conflict. Make an agreement with your partner that, unless otherwise stated, sexual fantasies are to be kept between you. Be a trustworthy confidante to your partner and honor your agreements. This creates the feeling of safety that allows for honest sharing.

Like any conversation about sex, be sensitive in your timing. Wait for your partner to feel relaxed so they have the free attention to give to this conversation. You might even plan a time to sit down and share fantasies. Planning for a conversation about fantasies can give you time to think about what you'll share and build some anticipation for a playful conversation. Remember that it may be hard for your partner to share some of their fantasies. Listen attentively and never judge or shame.

When you understand your partner's inner experience, you can help support and even create the kind of sex that lights them up. Whether it's sensual and romantic or kinky and complex, we can learn to meet our partner's core erotic needs.

Step 1: Self-acceptance

"Sometimes I fantasize about _____. Is that normal?"

Clients often look for reassurance that their fantasies fall within an acceptable norm. They sometimes feel confused about the fantasies that arouse them. Fantasies are born from a lifetime of experiences that have both opened us up and closed us down. Our erotic minds draw from all of it, and in the throes of sexual desire, these thoughts, imaginings, and scenarios can flood our brain. Talk openly about your fantasies and stay curious and accepting about whatever those fantasies are. Self-acceptance is the first step in being able to share sexual fantasies with your partner. There's nothing sexier than a confident lover who is sexually self-aware and shame-free.

Step 2: Tell the story

Pick your favorite erotic fantasy to share with your partner. If it doesn't have a particular story line, consider what that story line might be. Flesh it out in every detail, including the location, the conversation, your feelings, and every other detail. This helps your partner understand why you find it exciting. Our fantasies are clues to how our arousal system is wired. Our erotic mind communicates to us through imagery, which is indicative of the subconscious mind. Images evoke feelings, and if those feelings are eroticized in our brains, we seek those feelings to enhance our arousal. There's no limit to the types of feelings we can eroticize.

Step 3: Be curious

Invite your partner to ask questions and explore the origins of your fantasy. When do you remember first having this fantasy? Was the fantasy born out of a happy experience or a challenging experience? Be open to whatever information comes out of this investigation, and the reason why this fantasy has taken its place as one of your favorites. In my e-book *Your Erotic Menu* I offer readers a checklist of erotic activities and have columns for *yes*, *maybe*, and *fantasy*. I gave fantasy its own column because there may be many activities that turn us on mentally that in reality we would never want to actually do. This is an important distinction, not only for our *own* investigation but for our partner to know that we can be excited by a fantasy without ever expecting (or even wanting) to play it out for real.

Taking action on fantasies is another conversation. In the life outside of our brain, we take things into consideration, like our values, morals, belief systems, and accountability to others. Cause and effect may be the law outside of our mind, but in our heads we have free reign to explore.

"I don't fantasize and never have."

Not everyone identifies with having a fantasy life. Some people are less visual in their mental imaginings. Their erotic experience may be more physically focused. Scenarios or stories may be harder for them to identify. Don't force it. Rather, let yourself daydream. Give yourself the actual space and time to do nothing but wander in your mind. It's a rare indulgence these days.

If sexual fantasies don't come easily to you, you might remember past experiences of heightened arousal or movies with sexual scenes that stuck with you over the years. Erotic literature can also lead us into exciting scenarios, and it leaves lots of room for our imagination to fill in the rest.

Masturbation can lead us into mental imagery and scenarios that heighten our arousal. Next time you're having solo sex, pay attention to where your erotic mind leads you as your body moves toward orgasm.

"I don't want to betray my partner in my thoughts."

Fantasies don't have to involve other people (real or imagined). Many of my clients tell me their favorite fantasies are about their partner. They imagine a past sexual experience that was full of passion. They might fantasize about novel ways of relating to them, like dominance and submission. They might enjoy imagining their partner with a stranger or themselves with another person. You don't have to leave your partner behind in your fantasy world. Bring them along and give them a starring role!

"What if our fantasies are different?"

Chances are the nature of your fantasies will be different from those of your partner. You might get turned on by romantic lovemaking, and your partner may get turned on by power exchange and kink. That's okay. We can learn to acknowledge our differences without making our partner wrong. Once we understand the feelings and desires we're hoping for from sex, we can take turns visiting each other's preferred sexual experiences.

If you've gone through the exercise of sharing your erotic fantasies with each other, you now have the information you need to feed their fantasy back to them during sex. Part of being a good lover is being able to expand beyond our preferences and meet our lovers in their world as well. If you know your partner is turned on by romantic seduction, step into your inner seducer to give them that energy. If your partner's fantasy involves being dominant, set the stage for them to take charge and connect to the part of you that wants to let go and surrender.

"I want to be present when I have sex."

Sexual fantasies shouldn't be a replacement for presence. If you check out from your partner by getting lost in your mind, they'll feel it. Don't abandon your partner in the bedroom. Share your fantasy with them.

Make one up together just for fun. Use fantasy as a tool to strategically ramp up your turn-on when the time is right. Some people use fantasy in order to reach orgasm or heighten their orgasmic experience. Some use fantasy to get them in the mood for sex when their minds are elsewhere. We can move in and out of fantasy in ways that work for us without abandoning our partner.

By bringing attention to our sexual fantasies, we're investigating our erotic minds and the reasons we turn to sex in the first place. Our fantasies point the way to our core desires, and our core desires point the way to a fulfilling sexual life. Again,

- start by first investigating your favorite/familiar fantasies;
- accept your fantasies without shame or apology;
- share your fantasies in detail with your partner; and
- get curious about your fantasy's origins and embedded feelings.

43.

Bring Me A Higher Love:
Cannabis for Intimacy and Connection

I won't say exactly how long cannabis has been in my life, but the release of *Dark Side of the Moon* and my first joint fell in the same calendar year! I feel like a relic of the past when I remember terminology like *doobie*, *roach clip*, and *head shop*. That was also the year my sexuality came fully into being. Ergo, the idea of combining consciousness-altering substances with sensual pleasure is not new to me.

Cannabis is being legalized across the United States and in other countries, taking its rightful seat at the table of other health and wellness enhancement medicines. We no longer have to feel like criminals when we indulge in this sacrament; we can actually have a grown-up conversation about what's available in the realm of entheogens. And as a sex and intimacy coach, I'm particularly excited to share openly about how you can use cannabis to heighten your sensuality and partner intimacy.

Losing your mind

When it's time to be in your body rather than your head, I hope you can answer "yes" as in, "Yes, I've lost my mind!" In a recent questionnaire for my readers, roughly half answered in the affirmative when asked if they were too preoccupied with negative thoughts to let go and enjoy themselves sexually. Being *stuck in our heads* during sex and sensuality is a top challenge for both men and women. All that thinking and overthinking can undermine our openness to closeness with our partner.

Let's look at the notable ingredients of cannabis: THC and CBD. The levels of these two compounds will dictate the effect of cannabis on your intimate experiences and bodily pleasures.

CBD refers to a class of compounds that offer health benefits but generally don't alter your mood or mental state. CBD potions and remedies are available for a wide variety of health concerns. Of course, cannabis-derived products are available to address these concerns. They contain different proportions of THC and CBD, including zero THC content and different levels.

THC is the component that makes you feel "high" or "stoned," and is the main ingredient we can harness to enhance sex. With a little research and experimentation, you can determine your optimal level of THC. The "right dose" will relieve the chronic overthinking that leads to *anxiety* — the number one enemy of sexual performance and satisfying orgasms. Too much THC can make you feel sluggish, dissociated, and even a little paranoid (among other effects). A suitable "Goldilocks dose" (neither too big or too small) will elevate your mood and expand your perspective. Note that today's cannabis shops offer dozens of strains from which to choose. Each has its own subtle qualities, like wine varietals, but generally speaking they break into categories of Indica — which tend to offer a heavier body load (the feeling of being "stoned") — and Sativa — which is more of a head trip. Sativa is valued by aficionados for expanding creativity or even boosting energy. With Indica you might be inclined to lie on the couch and listen to an album; with Sativa, you could find yourself improvising on a musical instrument, or tidying the house!

What's best for you and your partner will vary from person to person and couple to couple. Indica might be your thing, or Sativa, or a blend. Some prefer to smoke it; others prefer so-called *edibles*. If this is all new to you, start with small amounts and seek a good "set and setting" as they say in psychedelic communities. Please be aware that cannabis doesn't agree with everyone, and you must check its legal status in your jurisdiction. I certainly don't wish to be seen as encouraging people to break the law in their locality.

Our society has condoned the use of alcohol for eons to settle us down, take the "edge off," and to function as a social lubricant. Personally, I don't feel that alcohol (other than in very small amounts) lends itself to intimacy, for a variety of reasons. Alcohol can lead to nausea. It's physically addictive which may lead to substance abuse and conflict. And when it comes to sex, alcohol impairs performance by numbing sensations and dulling our mental and situational awareness. (Not to mention the toxic after-effects of hangovers.)

Cannabis, on the other hand, brings us into the present moment and focuses our attention. It stimulates desire and creative thinking, and it enhances feelings of connection. It increases the intensity of our physical sensation and heightens the quality of our orgasms!

Again, the secret in using any consciousness-altering substance is *experimentation* and *moderation*. If you want connection, don't get so high that you can't be present and attuned to your partner! Please be a *grown up* and a *responsible* sexual partner. Start with small amounts and increase until you discover your optimal state for intimacy with a partner or intimacy with yourself.

And if you don't want the "higher" love, that's okay too! (Of course.) Cannabis is simply an option that some people enjoy for certain life-affirming qualities that have traditionally not enjoyed the publicity they deserve. With the advent of medical grade cannabis and low-dose THC, we can also get the health benefits of cannabis without the buzz.

Choose your strain of cannabis based on how you want to feel. Many people will find a hybrid of Indica and Sativa a good starting place for their experimentation. Too much of one and you're sleeping on the couch. Too much of the other and you feel more anxious than usual. Note that you can enjoy some of the sexual benefits of cannabis without feeling high! If you purchase low-THC cannabis products that are nevertheless rich in CBD compounds, the latter can create more blood flow to the genitals and increase nerve sensitivity. CBD can relax tense pelvic floor muscles and reduce vaginal pain and erection challenges. Cannabis with high levels of CBD also eases symptoms of menopause, mood swings, sleep disturbances, and even bone loss. So it's not all about the gifts of THC!

Questions to ask include: How do I want to feel? What am I using it for? Am I primarily looking to get high? And if so, *how high*? What's my preferred method of consuming cannabis? Smoking the flower? Vaping it? Eating it? Or applying creams, spraying oils, or using suppositories? Do I prefer Indica, Sativa, or a blend? All these choices will impact your experience. Don't be shy at cannabis stores and dispensaries. The staff are usually knowledgeable and happy to recommend products with names like Bubblegum Kush, Sour Diesel, Blue Dream, Love Potion #1, and so on. Don't be nervous, either, about asking for something that's good for sex and intimacy. You're not the only one asking, and these people have heard it all before!

44.

Eight Tips to Create an Awesome Date Night: A Peek Through the Bedroom Keyhole!

Ever wonder what happens in someone else's bedroom? We all do, right?

Consider this your "digital keyhole" into the bedroom of Ed and Carol, one of my coaching couples, and how they applied some of the coaching tips they received from me over a period of a few weeks. Then I'll break down all eight coaching tips they used on their date night so you can learn from them as well.

Heeding my advice, Ed and Carol planned when and where they were going to have some intimate time. They decided on a midweek evening, after the kids were settled down and the house was quiet. Ed told Carol there were some *rules* to their engagement that evening. They were to both dress up for each other. Ed asked Carol to put on something sexy and see-through so he could appreciate her body and said he would dress however she wished.

Ed asked that once they crossed the threshold of their bedroom that evening, no casual conversation occur about work, news, kids, money, or other day-to-day matters. Their conversation was to be about their relationship, their shared plans, their sexual turn-ons, or present-time feelings – in other words, subjects that create connection and intimacy.

Ed brought his computer into the bedroom so they could look at some sex toys; each of them could purchase something they'd like to introduce into their sexual play together. Ed took the initiative to dim the lights, put on some music, and prepare a favorite drink for Carol. There were no expectations other than conversation and sharing some intimate time. They could become sexual or not depending on their moods. When things ended up progressing over to the bed, Ed's earlier issues with ED disappeared. Ed suggested some explorations with spanking and sensation play, which they'd never tried before but about which both were curious.

The next day we all got on the phone to talk about their experience, and I praised them for all the small changes they made to make their time together not just good, but awesome! Let's look at the eight reasons why Ed and Carol had a great date night:

1. Ed and Carol both agreed to schedule a day when they could share some intimate time together. Planning sex sets you up for a good experience. They were both prepared, showered, and shaved. And they had some time to anticipate their upcoming date.

2. Ed had a sense of how he wanted their time together to go, so he and Carol both agreed that he'd plan that evening. With Ed taking charge, Carol could relax and follow his lead. This created the kind of sexual polarity that helped fuel their attraction and desire.

3. Ed gave Carol a clear and simple request to wear something specific that he liked, which gave Carol a tangible action to perform. She also appreciated knowing that Bob wanted to

see her body in something sexy. His request helped her feel attractive and desired.

4. Ed stated his boundaries by requesting that their conversation be restricted to subjects that fostered intimacy. All other subjects of conversation were left outside of the bedroom for that night.

5. Ed brought his computer into the bedroom for the sole purpose of looking at some online sex toy stores — to help them both connect to and share their desires. He also gifted Carol with any toy she wanted to purchase, which made her feel cared for.

6. Being the one who chose to lead, Ed took responsibility for creating a sensual space before Carol arrived. He changed the light bulb to a red one, he found some music he knew she'd like, and had their drinks ready when she entered the bedroom.

7. He also led her over to the couch rather than the bed so they could spend some time talking and sharing. Ed didn't have any issues with ED that night, which he'd been experiencing since he'd entered his fifties. He realized that taking the time to share and connect before sex was exactly what his body needed to become aroused.

8. They both agreed there was no expectation about whether sex would happen or not, so neither of them felt pressured to please or perform if the feeling wasn't there. They wanted their actions to follow their desires in the moment rather than have expectations or assumptions that sex would happen. As it turned out, they *did* both get turned on, and as things started to escalate, Ed suggested they try something new. He asked Carol if she'd be interested in some sensation play and spanking. This introduced some novelty into their sexual play and allowed them to see new sides of each other — sides that were more

playful and experimental. It also underscored the sexual polarity they were already feeling through Ed's directive leadership, and Carol's state of surrender and willingness to be led.

BONUS TIP: The next day the three of us met on Zoom to talk about how well the date night went and why. We talked about *what* worked and *why* it worked for them. They learned about each other's favorite moments and what they might want more of next time. They also enjoyed reliving and sharing their evening with me, because talking about sex can be fun, liberating and confidence building. I praised them for the choices they made to create a date night that was a great success on all eight counts.

When I watch my coaching couples move from disconnection and frustration to becoming reengaged and turned on, I see how everything they sought was already within them. They just needed to do the work to find their way back to presence, passion and pleasure.

BOOK THREE:
TURN ON

In the journey of long-term love and passion, few aspects of a relationship hold as much potential for connection and fulfillment as the realm of sexual intimacy. Yet, for many couples, navigating the intricacies of fulfilling sex can be a journey fraught with uncertainty, inhibition, and frustration.

In this section, we embark on a voyage of exploration, shedding light on the secrets to cultivating a deeply satisfying and fulfilling sexual connection. From communication and vulnerability to pleasure and new adventures, let's look at the essential elements that pave the way to becoming a Turned-On Couple.

45.

An Elephant in the Room:
How to Talk About S-E-X

We all lived through a pandemic. World-wide, couples were forced to stop everything – stop working, shopping, partying, gathering, vacationing, and dining out. Let's face it, we were forced to stop distracting ourselves; strip away distractions and we're suddenly confronted with the low-level stress that's driving us to distraction in the first place. We were forced to stop seeking outside of ourselves, which made space to start looking inside: our world of feelings, needs, emotions, and desires.

If we believe we can't change what's missing in our relationship, it makes perfect sense to ignore what's missing, deny the effect on us, and justify inaction. But living in denial and inaction comes at a price: intimacy. And what we lose in intimacy we gain in *resentment* and *disconnection*.

If you're living and sleeping with someone for whom you feel resentment and from whom you feel disconnected, I guarantee you're living with stress that's presenting itself in multiple ways daily. You may find yourself losing patience easily, snapping, withholding affection, and viewing your partner as an adversary rather than a teammate.

One way you might cope with a loss of intimacy is by constructing a story. You tell yourself that you don't want to *pressure your partner*. You don't want to be *selfish*. You've been living without for so long, you've gotten *used to it*. Talking about sex and intimacy might *rock the boat*. Living with these kinds of narratives accomplishes two things: you suppress your needs and desire for intimacy, and you disempower yourself from creating change.

Let's stop ignoring the "elephant in our relationship" and start talking about it. We can even thank the elephant for sticking around and reminding us that we're ignoring our own sensual and sexual needs.

Ask yourself: What are my sexual and sensual needs? What would it look like to have them met? How do I want to be seen and accepted in my sexuality? Who am I as a sexual being and what do I actually want?

We all acknowledge that to keep anything alive in our life we need to give it attention. We need to continue learning and growing. We need to invest ourselves and bring energy to it. We do this in our work. We do it in our play. We do it with our health and fitness, but for some reason we believe that our sexuality is an *exemption* to the rule!

We start having sex as teens (usually), and normally learn how to do it with one or more partners. Eventually we get together with someone and settle down in a long-term relationship and agree to the same kind of sex (usually) for years on end with the expectation that sex will remain interesting and fulfilling. However, thinking that good sex doesn't require attention, communication, and new learning is a *myth*, perhaps taught to us by romance novels, movies, and misinformed sex education.

So where to begin? Initiate a conversation about your desires between the three of you: you, your partner, and the elephant. Stop ignoring what's not being spoken, and welcome a conversation about sex and sensuality. When you approach this conversation from a loving place of listening, curiosity, open-hearted exploration, and patience, you'll invite in the intimacy you've lost along the way.

Eight ground rules for talking about sex

If you've been silently suffering an unsatisfying sex life, the path to sexual fulfillment starts by learning to express your desires. I'm fully aware this can be a daunting task so let me offer you a few helpful tips on how to make it go as smoothly as possible. Whether you're in a long-term relationship or currently dating, you can learn to talk about sex as comfortably as you would about where to go for lunch.

Ask your partner for some time to sit down to talk about your intimate life when you're not in bed. Choose a relaxed time and place. (I use the words "intimate life" because sex is more than just a physical act; it's an act of intimacy, no matter what kind of sex you're having. So inviting your partner to talk about your intimate life telegraphs that you want to find connection. You want to feel their body close to yours and feel the love that comes from sexual connection.)

If things have been less than satisfactory for a while, conversations about sex are often full of blame and guilt (whether spoken or unspoken). You might feel your partner tense up at first or get defensive as they brace for the negative emotions this subject may have brought up in the past. Here are eight ways to ease their defensiveness:

1. Be patient and stay with them as they find their comfort with the conversation.

2. Reassure your partner that you want to talk about your intimate life in a way that's open-hearted. You want to hear their needs and be curious about solutions that work for both of you. Show them they can trust you to be honest.

3. Acknowledge what you love about your partner. Help them relax and feel appreciated. Express gratitude. Make a list of all the ways they make your life better so they're fresh in your mind. How long has it been since you've spoken words of gratitude?

4. Be specific when you ask for what you want more of. Don't presume your partner doesn't like a certain activity if you've never actually talked about it. Don't try to intuit what you think your partner wants; ask them directly and listen to their requests.

5. Stay away from presumptions about what your partner might be feeling. You're not a mind reader, and what they may have expressed in the past doesn't mean they feel that way now. Ask them to share their feelings so you hear it from them.

6. Focus your side of the conversation on your feelings rather than blaming or pointing a finger. If your partner has turned you down sexually for a while, confess how that makes you feel. "When you turn down my invitations, I feel rejected/alone/sad/abandoned." Don't be afraid to be vulnerable with your feelings as this invites them to do the same. Avoid statements that you know might trigger your partner. Before speaking, ask yourself this very important question: "Is what I'm about to say going to create connection or disconnection?"

7. Make eye contact and be present. Take turns talking and then listening. Don't defend yourself or interrupt. Repeat back what you heard them say. "What I hear you saying is that you feel like I only show affection when I want sex, is that right?" When they hear you say it back to them, your partner will feel heard and understood. It takes courage to open up about sex, so thank them for sharing and show your appreciation.

8. Breathe and relax. Lead with confidence and presence. If your energy is relaxed and grounded, they will follow your lead.

Share these ground rules with your partner. By agreeing to them you make space for conversations about sex that will leave you both feeling heard and accepted.

46.

Why Have Sex?
The Importance of Finding Your "Whys"

We're all on a wild ride together. There's no question about that. Every part of our lives — including health, politics, cultural norms, and the environment — is in crisis. Depression and anxiety are skyrocketing. I don't know about you, but it sometimes feels like life is spinning out of control. When I sit down to write about sex, or speak to a group, a coach, or a client, the question, "Why have sex?" keeps bubbling up. Even in ordinary times it's important to answer this question, but especially so these days.

Let's look at some of the roles sex plays in our lives and why now — more than ever — sexual intimacy can support our health and well-being.

Intimacy and biology

Intimacy is my number one reason for keeping sex alive (and fulfilling) during stressful times. That applies to partner sex and solo sex. Feeling intimate is a basic human need. Sexual intimacy is a uniquely potent manifestation of that. It requires us to open and share our bodies as well as our hearts. Being seen by our partner in our desire and orgasmic energy is extremely intimate and vulnerable. We feel seen, accepted, and wanted. These experiences feed our hearts and souls, and all these feelings help regulate us emotionally. When we're emotionally replenished with expressions of intimacy, we're better able to meet the world's demands with balance, calm and clarity.

Similarly, being sexually active and fulfilled impacts our self-esteem. Feeling loved up and satisfied brightens our day and how we relate to work, parenting, and the world. Everyone in our life benefits from our sexual satisfaction!

From hormones to neurotransmitters, sex creates states of relaxation and closeness that can impact a relationship for days afterwards. One female client says the closeness she and her partner feel after sex is her "why" for having sex in the first place. She sees the difference it makes in her partner's state of happiness and mood, as well as her own. This positively impacts how she views her partner, which in turn enhances his feelings of love and acceptance for her. The wheels go around and round. Orgasms don't just feel good in the moment: they also help protect us from depression and anxiety. So, partnered or solo, it's healthy to include orgasms in your mental fitness routine.

Sex as a health and wellness practice

Those same hormones bolster our immune system, helping us to ward off illness. Sex also reduces stress. Chronic stress is endemic in our crazy world. Its damage touches every part of our human body and brain and can lead to conditions such as high blood pressure. Sexual intimacy and orgasmic release reset our nervous system and return us to a much-needed state of peace.

Sex is a pain reliever. Stepping out of the contraction of pain and turning our attention to pleasure may shift brain chemistry and alter one's experience of pain. Sex helps us sleep better, too! It's an accepted fact that sex reduces heart attacks and strokes. Having sex is on par with a brisk walk or light exercise, and it's a lot more fun.

All this is to say, find your "why's" for keeping sex interesting and desirable — and remember them! Sex isn't just for the stress-free, the turned on, or the wild explorers; sex is for every human. Sexuality is an integral part of who we are born to be. It's a magical concoction of brain chemistry, hormones, and our nervous system mixed with so much vulnerability, love, and intimacy that it calms and soothes a worried mind.

Use sex to enhance your life emotionally, physically, psychologically, and spiritually. Put sex to use in ways that extend and enliven your quality of life. If sex has become predictable (intercourse and orgasm driven) or another task to cross off your to-do list, It's time to learn and grow together.

47.

I'm Done with Sex!
Out with the Old. In with the New.

This chapter is for a subsection of women, and the people who want to understand those women better.

A therapist friend of mine once asked me if many of the women I work with ever confess that they're just done with sex. My answer was, "yes." They've had the babies and many years of sex with their partners. They've never felt very sexual — it was never that important to them.

They're done!

When I hear a woman make such a resounding statement, I imagine a long road of frustration, obligation, unmet desires, and unspoken words leading up to that absolute declaration. Sex is not about obligation, although women have been told this for eons. Until relatively recently women were considered the property of men. A woman's role in life was to have a family and solely support her husband's goals. In many parts of the world this remains the case. In my own lifetime, a woman had to get her husband's signature to get a credit card. Women weren't allowed to serve on a jury or have access to Ivy League education! The list goes on.

It's helpful to keep these facts in perspective as we look at the role sex plays in many women's lives.

Birth control, access to abortion, planned parenthood, marriage of choice, jobs outside the home, financial independence, consent conversations, female sexual pleasure — all are (relatively speaking) game-changers for women's independence and their relationship to sex. It's only been one generation since girls walked out of sex education with two takeaways:

1. Keep your legs closed if you don't want to get pregnant, and
2. Boys only want one thing. (In other words, fend off the aggressors or your life will be ruined.)

Desire, pleasure, seduction, and intimacy were not part of the sexual curriculum or conversation. Boys weren't taught how to be good lovers, and girls resigned themselves to whatever happened. This was usually unfulfilling, due to the lack of understanding of the female body (and soul).

These days, women may consciously understand that sex is more than simply an *obligation* to keep a relationship intact. Times have changed, right? Not according to the numbers, sadly. Low libido (or lack of interest in sex) is present in 26.7 percent of premenopausal women, and 52.4 percent of post-menopausal women.

Is it a woman's nature to be less interested in sex — especially as she ages – or is it the kind of sex she's having that leaves her cold?

If sex is just intercourse focused with minimal mental, emotional, and physical foreplay, a woman's inherent nature won't be engaged, nor will the pleasure centers throughout her body that awaken arousal. If she's not educated to view sex as a source of her own pleasure, she'll lack the tools — and even the inclination — to identify what she wants in sex and to ask for it from a partner. If the way a woman experiences sex doesn't open her to connection and intimacy (whatever style of sex she's having), she'll eventually become resigned to feeling sex is more for her partner than for her.

Women are raised to be good at giving, at putting other's needs first, but applying those skill sets to sex can eventually lead to low sexual interest and even resentment. Obligatory sex isn't just unsatisfying for women; it's equally unsatisfying for their partners. I often hear men express their longing to feel desired by their partners.

Women and men are learning as we go. Every generation is evolving our sexual awareness. Relatively speaking, we're still in the early days of a sex education that represents female pleasure. Women's sexual empowerment is now part of the conversation. We're all doing the best we can to wake up to the mistakes and inequalities of previous generations. But, behind the bedroom doors, conscious and subconscious attitudes and beliefs still linger. After all, we were raised by parents who were influenced by their parents and so on.

If you understand intergenerational trauma, you know that trauma experienced in one generation affects the health and wellbeing of descendants. This intergenerational download is almost all subconscious. Ninety percent of our brain is a subconscious collection of unintentional thoughts, behaviors, and actions. How many women were

- indoctrinated into saying "no" to sex from a young age?
- taught to hate their bodies based on societal standards of the time?
- raised to believe that female sexual pleasure isn't important enough to speak up about?
- told that to be a good wife, they should put their husband's pleasure above their own?
- called a "slut" and socially ostracized by their peers if they appeared to enjoy sex too much?

- faking orgasms or *performing* to please a partner? or
- never taught how to talk about sex with confidence and clarity?

Early messages about female sexuality combined in our subconscious minds to create confusion and ambivalence around our own sexuality. When I hear a woman say she's *done* with sex, I hear her saying she's done with a sexual paradigm that may have never worked for her in the first place. She's done feeling disconnected from her body and desires. She's done with a lack of intimacy. She's done with hardening herself to the belief that sex is not meant for her pleasure. In other words, she's done with sex *as it is.*

In such instances I hope that being *done* can be transformed from an ending into a beginning. While one door closes, another can open. Walking through that door can be a vulnerable journey. A woman might need to transmute her resentment into a reengagement with pleasure — a discovery of her own sexual empowerment outside the societal messages with which she grew up. Can she learn to identify her sexual desires? Can she embrace sex as an integral part of her womanhood, to be shared and celebrated?

I certainly hope so. My coaching practice has taught me that at least in a percentage of cases, being *done with sex* is a reaction to an unworkable situation. Ever evolving is the desire to act toward something better. If you or your partner are part of this subsection of women who've emotionally disconnected from sex, starting to talk about sex is where it all begins. Share this chapter with one another and open up about your sexual histories. Ask each other questions about what it was like growing up:

- "What were the messages you received (verbal or nonverbal) about sex, masturbation, and nudity?"
- "How were you conditioned by the attitudes of family or friends?"

- "How did you learn about sex (and how do you *wish* you'd learned about sex)?"
- "What are your early memories of sexual feelings and experimentation?"

Understanding our partner's relationship to sex, based on their life history, is an invaluable part of a vibrant sex life. Be a good listener. Don't judge or try to "fix" them. Change occurs when we feel safe to share and we feel accepted, even with our limitations.

48.

Can We Talk?
Talking About Sex with Your Partner

"We haven't had sex in months. This is not what I signed up for when we got together five years ago!"

These words from a past client ring in my head now and then, when I think about couples who are dissatisfied with their sex lives. You can feel the utter frustration he felt when it came to his unmet expectations. Over those five years, his experience of his sex life changed or — more than likely — the conversation about sexual compatibility never occurred. This is often the case in new relationships when things are novel and exciting.

He wasn't experiencing what was important to him or, in other words, he and his partner didn't share the same sex and intimacy values.

"Have you and your partner ever explicitly discussed what's important to each of you when it comes to sex and intimacy?" I asked him. "What do you both value in your experience together?"

Have *you* ever talked with your partner about what's important to each of you in your sexual and intimate life together? When you ask and answer these questions, you can explore how to harmonize your values and get your expectations met. If your values differ (which is often the case), the question arises: How do you accommodate those differences?

Sex is one of the most difficult topics of conversation for couples. I'd like to offer you a framework to guide your exploration and ease things a bit.

Identify and rank your sex and intimacy values

I've listed some of the values that could be part of your preferred experience of sex and intimacy. Feel free to add to this list. Note which ones stand out to you. Maybe you want them all. (I do!) For this exercise, write down your top five.

- Physical affection (cuddling, hugging, PDAs, and hand holding, for example)
- Presence (present moment attentiveness, listening with interest)
- Passion (letting go into desire, taking and being taken)
- Sensuality (touching for pleasure, massage, sensation exploration)
- Spontaneity (unplanned sexy time, initiating through surprise or opportunity)
- Planned sex (setting a day and time, putting it on the schedule, prioritizing sex)
- Playfulness (humor, laughter, lightness, games, letting your inner child out to play)
- Depth (going deep, expressing emotions, feeling deeply)
- Sacredness (connecting to something greater in your union, bringing in spirit as part of your experience, rituals that give meaning to your sexuality)
- Kink (exploring limits, fetishes, power exchange, role play, different sexual personas)
- Quantity (wanting sex often, regularity, believing that more is better)

- Quality (making sex special, going for the gold, wanting the best each time)
- Tenderness (loving care, kindness, protection)
- Boldness (directness, asking for what you want)
- Confidence (stepping into your sexiness, feeling sure of who you are)
- Surrender (being led, handing over control, trusting, submitting)
- Loving (to feel loved completely, adored, devoted)
- Orgasms (pleasure based, making orgasm a priority, exploring different types of orgasms)
- Exploration and adventure (trying new things, being open to new things, novelty)
- Dominance (taking charge, leading, empowered)

Now that you've selected five from this list (or other items you added) your next task is to rank your top five sex and intimacy values in order from highest to lowest.

Get clear on what you need

Once you have your top five values sorted, consider the ways in which your partner can support those values in your sex life. Give yourself some time with this; communicating your values and needs is important, but considering how to *get your values and needs met* is the *real* conversation. Ask your partner to choose their top five values, on their own, by following the steps above, and then share them with you.

Here are some examples of how you could share your values, and how your partner could support you in giving you the kind of experience that's important to you:

Value: Confidence

"When you admire my body, I feel confident and sexy."

Value: Planned sex

"When you express how important sex is to you, it inspires me to plan for it, and put it in our schedule."

Value: Exploration and Adventure

"When you propose new experiences, it heightens my sense of exploration and adventure."

Include as much detail as possible about how your partner can support your top five values and how you can support theirs. And remember to avoid any blaming or complaining language, such as "you always..." or "you never..." There's no looking back; there's only moving forward! Talk as team players in making your sex and love life great for both of you. That requires kindness, curiosity, and acceptance.

49.

Sexual Shame 2.0:
A Generational Hand-Me-Down?

Here's my antidote to the silence of sexual shame:

Our culture is in a multi-decade "sexual revolution" that began in the 1960s, but we're far from being free from the deeply ingrained programming that sex is still a fundamentally shameful topic of conversation; beliefs persist that we unwittingly inherited from our parents (and their parents and their parents).

You might not identify with having sexual shame. Perhaps you're quite liberal when it comes to the sex you see on screen and in advertising. You could support honest and truthful sex education and have a tolerant, accepting attitude toward less conventional sexual expressions. However, the shame I'm talking about is found less in spoken opinions and more in *unspoken* feelings and beliefs.

Not wanting to talk about sex in our relationships is how we carry forth our ancestors' sexual doctrine, and I see it in many of my clients. Shame impacts how we conduct ourselves around sex: the conversations we're not willing to have with our partners, the changes we're not willing to make, and the risks we're not willing to take in order to have a fulfilling sex life (whatever fulfilling means to you). Sexual shame hides in the shadowy corners of the bedroom. It shows up as silence, secrecy, denial, and judgment.

Shame is the reason that 20 percent of committed long-term relationships become sexless. Sexual challenges are a major factor in half of all marriages ending in divorce. Conversations about sex don't take place often enough between partners. Excuses like boredom, distraction, and loss of interest are often used to avoid sex in relationships. Shame hides behind our resignation and our capacity to put up with something that doesn't work for us (for fear of rocking the relationship boat).

The sexual revolution may have led us to the land of sexual availability when it comes to dating, hookups, and onscreen sex, but it hasn't yet freed us enough to embrace the honest conversations that can lead to *sexual fulfillment*. This is where couples often fall short to the point of silence. Even therapists sometimes skirt around the subject of sex due to a lack of training in sexuality or their own discomfort with the subject. And so the "elephant in the office" sits silent and ignored.

If any other part of your life was threatening to end your relationship, you'd be sitting down as a team to talk about it. You'd figure it out. You'd fight for it. But because of *shame*, sex is a conversation into which many couples are afraid to enter, and partners remain alone in their personal struggle. Shame whispers in our ear with messages like:

- "I don't like sex. I'm broken."
- "I don't want to talk about sex. My partner should just know what to do."
- "My partner says I'm frigid or I'm a sex addict."
- "My abuse history was my fault."
- "If I want to stay married, I have to cope with living without sex."

- "I have to hide who I am from my partner; I know they wouldn't accept what turns me on."
- "The sex isn't great, but there's nothing we can do about it."

How does sexual shame operate in your life today? Are you still dragging along the remnants of sexual shame you inherited from your ancestors? We're all a product of past generations. We all grew up in homes that shaped our sexual beliefs, but sexuality is no longer simply a marital obligation to keep the peace and procreate. Human sexuality is always evolving, and our beliefs and attitudes can evolve as well.

The bodily pleasure and intimate connection we find in sex are important human needs. When we feel the truth of this, we can let go of our hand-me-down shame and rigid beliefs. We can bring more curiosity to our desires and, with that new-found curiosity, start an honest conversation with our partners about our needs and desires.

50.

Is It Time to "Marie Kondo" Your Sexual Beliefs?

A client told me she was doing a "Marie Kondo" on her closet, ridding herself of anything that no longer gave her joy. We went on to talk about her sex life with her partner that included a nagging resistance to being touched.

Somewhere along the line she formed a belief system about touch. She couldn't identify a particular incident that informed that belief system. There was no trauma or abuse. She just knew that when she was touched (even by her loving partner) her body would recoil, and she'd shut down.

This didn't stop her from having a sex life, but it did prevent her from looking forward to sex and enjoying it! After a few coaching sessions, she was ready to see her touch aversion for what it was: a belief system that no longer serves her. I suggested she view her beliefs much like the old sweaters she was throwing out and do a *Marie Kondo* on her sexual beliefs.

She could hold them up one at a time and ask, "Does this belief spark joy?" This isn't as easy as throwing out an old sweater, but it poses the same simple question. It became clear to her that she (and her body) believed receiving touch was not *joyful*. She packed up those beliefs and did the work of replacing them with beliefs that serve her.

I reminded her of Marie's very important step before letting something go, which is to first thank the belief for the place it held in your life and the purpose it served at the time. When we form beliefs about sex, we're usually pretty young. Our early life experiences often imprint themselves strongly in our brain. Everything is new, we're inexperienced, and we're easily influenced (in our attitudes). We form judgments and develop fears that can stay with us for a lifetime. That is, unless we hold them up to the light of scrutiny and ask ourselves Marie's question, Does this belief system spark joy?

Our most *troubling* and *constricting* beliefs could have protected us from hurt in the past. Our judgments and fears may have actually *kept us safe* at one point in time! But if those beliefs no longer reflect who you are today and no longer protect you from a threat, then you have the choice to replace old beliefs with new ones.

So, rather than shoving your antiquated beliefs in a box of shame and regret, you can hold them up to the light and give them a final look. Ask yourself: What are my antiquated sexual beliefs? Is it time to open the closet door and update what's inside?

51.

Growing Up with Sex:
One Decade at a Time

For most of us, sex takes up a huge amount of our brain's bandwidth throughout our lives. (Allow me to generalize a bit here, keeping in mind that sexuality is a unique path for any individual.) As teenagers, many of us stumble through a decade of infatuations, fantasies, and hormonal-driven preoccupations with bodily pleasure (solo and partnered). We're assessing our physical attractiveness and comparing our bodies and looks to other people's standards. Most of our sexual explorations come in the form of awkward experimentation, infused with self-doubt. We're both innocently dependent on approval and stubbornly independent of unsolicited advice.

We spend our twenties and thirties seeking sexual experience, building confidence, and (for a lot of us) hoping for long-term love and fulfillment. Sex may be front and center in our attention. We might dig deeper into our sexuality and open ourselves to new sexual expressions.

In those decades we peak energetically and are biologically prepped to procreate. We talk about sex with our friends. We attempt to construct an empowered sexual identity. And — if sex is important to us — we do our best to ensure that it's a priority in our lives and relationships.

By the time we reach our forties and fifties, we may feel more pressure from outside demands. If we're partnered, we do our best to ensure that sex and pleasure don't fall off the schedule. However, the demands of parenting and paying bills might erode our youthful sexual appetite. A midlife crisis, an affair, sexual exploration — all these add fuel or drama to our sexual experience. What was once our body's predictable sexual desire shifts to something less familiar. Couples try to make sex a priority, but it can become *yet another task* slotted into one long busy schedule.

Sex in our sixties and beyond contends with physical changes that can take us in one of two directions. Changes in our desire and bodies can either shut sex down or invite us into new experiences of an ever-evolving nature. The hormonal bodies that so urgently ushered us into puberty now lead us by the hand into our later years. The purpose of sex over sixty shifts from biologically driven procreation to new frontiers of intimacy and physical pleasure.

Every decade serves us up a unique sexual buffet of experience and challenges, doesn't it? We mature emotionally, physically, intellectually, and spiritually; if we want sex to remain an integral part of our lives, we make sex part of our conversation to ensure that sex matures right along with us. At least, *that's the idea*.

The success of our evolution depends on our willingness to do the personal work — to understand our blocks and resistance – and acceptance of *change* as part of our *sexual journey* (through an ever-shifting landscape). Our sexual tastes mature, our desires express themselves differently, and our body's arousal and responses change. Sex isn't just one thing that starts in our teens and stays the same! Our sexuality grows and matures throughout our lives.

If we resist change — such as the level of sexual desire in a long-term relationship — we're not examining what's possible *now*. For instance, we might pull away from sex because our ability to, say, have an orgasm or maintain an erection is suddenly not what it was before. We're in unfamiliar territory, and we could miss the opportunity to learn more about pleasure and all its variations. We can experience self-doubt about our changing bodies and then find excuses to shut sex down.

Ask yourself: Where am I in the life cycle of my sexuality? What phase am I in?

Sit down with your partner and talk about your sexual evolution through the decades. What did sex mean to you as a teen? How did it evolve as you matured into an adult? What was it like when you first met each other, and how did you see things progress? What phase is your sexuality in now, *as a couple*?

When we honestly address our relationship with our sexuality, we open up and share a deeper side of ourselves. There's no shame in admitting that our sexuality changes or that our bodies feel different. Stay open and honest and avoid blame or judgment. Get curious about your partner and what they have to say. Ask questions that draw them out and help them feel safe. View every decade as a new sexual frontier with challenges to embrace and lessons to learn.

52.

Thoughts on Sexual Savoring: For Pleasure's Sake

There are places on my daily walk where I pick a small lavender bud to crush in my hands and inhale its calming fragrance. I pass a running creek that sparkles in the sun. I see dogs of all kinds engaged in their own present-moment practice. I see white clouds appearing and disappearing and vibrant colors in changing leaves.

If I'm aware enough to notice these opportunities to slow down and see what's in front of me, I take a breath and remind myself to "savor." *Savoring* is more than mindfulness. Mindfulness brings us to a razor's edge of awareness that has qualities of neutrality and acceptance. Mindfulness teaches us to be with *what is*. Savoring brings an additional layer of experience. It brings a depth of noticing that's filled with gratitude and appreciation, and even a sense of preciousness.

We all have our moments where we fully receive the gift of what's there to be savored, knowing that every moment is fleeting and therefore precious. When I savor something, I imagine breathing it in completely, even combining with it like I'm squeezing out every ounce of pleasure from the experience.

Here are some savoring memories that come to mind: Standing in front of a brilliant sunset, immersing my nose in a bouquet of flowers, kissing a baby's belly, embracing a 2000-year-old redwood tree, cuddling up to a warm body, and feeling pride in myself and others. I can close my eyes and savor the memory.

Sexual savoring is the same as raising a rose to your nose and breathing deeply. Sexual savoring means slowing down and noticing what's happening — what's worthy of appreciation. As I say to my clients, even in moments when our needs aren't being perfectly met, there's almost always something worth savoring.

Sexual savoring is a mindset. It's a decision we make, and an action we take. Savoring takes us out of our heads and into our present-moment senses: the curve of your lover's hip, their voice in your ear, the beating of their heart, their laughter, their silence, the physical pleasure of sensations, and the excitement of building arousal.

So many small moments are worthy of stopping, noticing, and savoring before they're gone and replaced by the next moment! It's like mining for the threads of gold that run through a rock; we hold the rock up to the sun to see what's there to savor (in any moment).

When we feel the pleasure of someone's finger lightly traveling down our spine, we can allow ourselves to savor the experience. When we breathe in the scent of our partner's skin, we can connect to the pure pleasure of that breath. When we feel desire arise with a willing partner, we can remind ourselves to savor that moment and mark it in our memory as something precious and worth remembering.

Lovers who know how to savor are fully embodied in their sexual experience. They're present and attuned to the moment. They don't seek to get somewhere other than where they are. They connect to their desire and appreciation, and their partners feel it.

Welcoming our own pleasure and savoring isn't easy for everyone. Savoring may feel contrary to the messages we've told ourselves, messages like

- "I'm not worthy of sexual pleasure;"
- "I need to focus on my partner's pleasure more than my own;"
- "If I can't have the kind of sex life I want, then there's nothing in it for me;" and
- "I'm too distracted by more important things to fully enjoy myself."

Allowing ourselves to take pleasure and savor an experience labels that memory as positive. It supports our ability to, in Joseph Campbell's words, "follow our bliss" and notice where it wants to lead us.

If you accept that every moment offers something to savor, sex becomes a string of moments you can mine for their embedded gold. Savoring may not solve all our sexual challenges any more than smelling a lavender bud solves all of life's challenges, but it brings our focus to what's happening. It welcomes in the pleasure to be found and it empowers us to follow our own bliss. So, the next time you have sex (partnered or solo), slow down — for pleasure's sake — and remember to *savor*.

53.

Good Vibes:
Three Lessons Vibrators Taught Me
About Good Sex

My female cousin was a primary contributor to my early sex education when I needed it most. For instance, she clarified that I couldn't get pregnant by dancing with a boy, no matter how close we got. She also confirmed that I wasn't the only person who touched themselves (down there), and most importantly, she showed me that "wellness massagers" from Sears were used for things other than sore necks and shoulders.

A few years later my boyfriend introduced me to the real deal: A vibrator made specifically for genital arousal. It was a cream-colored, hard plastic, shapeless cylinder with a twisting on/off switch at the end. My first vibrator turned sex from an act I'd perform because my boyfriend liked it, into a sensual experience designed for my orgasmic pleasure.

Here are three lessons my first vibrator taught me about sexual pleasure:

1. Sexual pleasure is for me, not just my partner. Both genders come into sex with misconceptions and beliefs based either on inadequate sex education that doesn't address pleasure or on

porn that depicts male pleasure over female pleasure. When a young woman begins to experience sex for her own pleasure, she awakens her sexual desire. Owning her desire makes sex not only better for her, but it makes her a better lover for her partner as well.

2. Vibrators help me explore my own body and its unique paths to arousal. When I could give myself an orgasm, I felt more confident about having an orgasm with a partner. If a woman comes to me wanting to learn how to orgasm with her partner, I'll first coach her in how to get comfortable with masturbation and giving herself orgasms. Once she understands how her body works, she can show her partner how to touch her and how to please her.

3. I am in control of my orgasmic pleasure, and I don't need to rely on anyone else to give it to me. If a woman grows up always relying on a partner to have an orgasm, she can fail to develop a sense of healthy autonomy in relationships. A woman can share partner sex, but an orgasm is something a woman can give herself. Our bodies are made for sexual pleasure, whether we're partnered or not.

My first vibrator, many years ago, taught me these three important lessons about sexual pleasure and laid the foundation for all the other sex toys to come into my life, of which there have been many! I think back now on that shapeless, hard plastic, noisy vibrator that I thought was the best invention ever... We've come a long way, *baby!*

54.

A Slow Hand:
The Wisdom of Slowing Down

For a period of time there was a song I just couldn't get out of my head: It's the Pointer Sisters' song whose lyrics are:

> *"I want a man with a slow hand*
> *I want a lover with an easy touch*
> *I want somebody who will spend some time*
> *Not come and go in a heated rush*
> *I want somebody who will understand*
> *When it comes to love, I want a slow hand."*

This was written by a woman who knows what she wants and isn't afraid to ask for it. She wants a man who is going to take his time so she can relax and not feel rushed. She wants a slow hand so her body can warm up and become fully aroused. She wants to be ready to receive her lover into her body easily and without discomfort. And she knows what she needs for that to happen.

We're all raised on media depicting frantic lovers tearing their clothes off as fast as they can so they get to intercourse as quickly as possible and have an orgasm. Wham, bam, and it's over! If you asked the woman in that scene if that was good for her, she'd probably say she didn't have an orgasm and, overall, it happened too fast to really feel much of anything. She might even confess her moans were more for her partner's pleasure because she wasn't fully in her body enough to connect to her own desire. It was probably over before her genitals knew what was happening.

If you learned how to have hot sex by watching movies or porn, your sex education lacks the wisdom of slowing down and guiding your lover's body into an open, receptive, and pleasurable state. Slowing down with your lover is not just about *reducing speed*, it's about *gaining awareness*.

When we slow anything down — from eating to breathing to sexing — we notice much more information comes to us about what's happening in the moment. Slowing down isn't always an easy thing to do. Sometimes it requires real effort!

Allow me to make a quick segue to illustrate my point: The first time I visited Burning Man in the Nevada Desert, my partner and I arrived after dark; Black Rock City was in full throttle with music, lights, bikes, and people moving in every direction as far as you could see. My senses were overloaded! Signs along the road every few yards indicated the very strict 5 mph speed limit. After so many hours of traveling at 70 mph getting to the event, it was hard to drive for a mile or two at such a snail's pace! I found myself unconsciously speeding up and having to slow down repeatedly. But the slower I went the more I saw of this amazing environment. Once I got used to moving so slowly, I started noticing where I was and what I was traveling through. All my senses were engaged in what was happening around me. By the end of the week, a vehicle traveling 10 miles an hour seemed dangerously fast.

I had found a new normal. Likewise, we can find a new normal speed when it comes to sex and sensuality. Slowing down during sex connects us to a lot of information that we'd otherwise miss. We can gain access to that information by asking ourselves these questions:

- What's happening in our body? What is our body telling us? Does it feel tense or relaxed?
- Is there something that needs to happen to increase pleasure?
- What thoughts are going through our head? Are we having an anxious inner dialogue that's undermining our pleasure and presence?
- Are we picking up on our partner's signals about what they need to increase their enjoyment or feel more connection?
- Are we feeling our receptivity or noticing our resistance?
- Are we feeling each sensation or are we driving 60 miles an hour toward our orgasm?

By simply slowing down, all this information becomes more available. Your partner will notice how "in the moment" you've become. If you take the lead in your sexual connection, you can set the pace. Tell your partner you want to slow things down and savor each moment like you would if you were dining at a Michelin-starred restaurant. The next time you spend some intimate time with a lover, set the pace by taking some deep breaths and connecting to your body. If you're not sure how to do that, let me lead you through a simple embodiment practice:

- Stand up and start to shake your body. Shake it vigorously all over including your head, arms, hips, and legs. Shake all over for 60 seconds without stopping.
- Now close your eyes. (Be careful not to lose your balance.)
- Notice how you just completely changed your state within a minute of engaging with your body and moving some energy.

- Feel the vibration of peacefulness now that you're still. Notice your heart beating in your chest. You can even feel the blood coursing through your veins.
- Scan your body for any tension. Starting from your toes and moving upward, slowly bring your attention to each part of your body. Go slow enough to notice all the tiny muscles under the larger ones that may be holding tension, and then let them relax.
- Once you've reached the top of your head, face, and scalp, find a place in your body where you feel centered and grounded in your energy. For some that might be their pelvis or belly. For others, their heart and chest area.
- Breathe deeply into that place and feel the difference in your connection to what is happening below your neck, now that you've taken a moment to scan for tension and relax.
- Find that centered peaceful place in your body and return to that place any time you feel anxious or stuck in your head.

The next time you're with your partner, return to that centered place and breathe fully. Then, whatever you're doing together, slow it down. And then slow it down even more! And then even more than that! Notice what changes in your sensations, your connection to your partner, and your awareness of the present moment.

Being embodied and slowing down is the foundation to whatever kind of sex you're having, from Tantra to kink to vanilla sex. Sexual sensation happens in your body, so slow down enough to get into your body. And note that many beautiful exercises and practices (to explore the world of slow sex) can be applied to solo sex or partner sex.

55.

From "No" to "Yes":
Walking the Delicate Path

For a time, I was hooked on the Netflix reality show *Married at First Sight*. It followed four couples who agreed to arranged marriages, meeting for the first time on the day of their wedding. Three relationship experts paired them from a large pool of applicants. The show followed these four couples for a period of two months — from the honeymoon to sharing an apartment for eight weeks — as they worked on achieving success in their day-to-day lives as a married couple. At the end of the series, the couples decide if they want to stay together or get a divorce.

Crazy, right?

As a relationship and intimacy coach, I found it fascinating to watch these four couples do their best to achieve happiness together, with cameras on them for most of their waking hours! The challenges for each couple were different, but by the end of the series all four couples shared one problem: sex.

Within just a couple of months of marriage these four couples had each already established unhealthy patterns leading to disconnection. For the purpose of this chapter, I'll talk about two of the couples who dealt with a similar sexual dynamic. They were both struggling with *sexual resistance* — a dynamic I often encounter with my clients. (Sexual resistance can be defined as a developed pattern of "sex avoidance.")

Let's look at these two couples.

The first couple, both in their late twenties, had a lot in common except for the fact that the woman was a 27-year-old virgin, saving herself for her husband, and the man was more sexually experienced. I'm sure I wasn't the only person fascinated with this scenario! Here was a woman who, nearing thirty, placed great importance on *not* having sex before marriage and yet was marrying and living with a total stranger for two months!

It was painful to watch the tension she held in her body with any offering of sensuality or sexuality. She looked terrified to give up control and engage in intimacy of any kind. I felt bad for her that she now had to undo years of being in sexual shutdown, with no learned skills on how to access her own desire, then show that desire to her husband.

And I felt bad for him, too, dealing with an emotionally and sexually inexperienced wife with an extreme amount of resistance to his patient advances. Looking past the unusual circumstance of living with a camera crew, the signs of their struggle were obvious and this was supported by the individual interviews as well.

The second couple had a similar dynamic, in that the 29-year-old woman had not been in a relationship for 10 years (since college). She struggled with being vulnerable and deflected his compliments and affection, even though she described him as her perfect match. This resistance created polarity between them.

This man, as with the first couple, was also very patient. He would tiptoe around the edge of her comfort zone, hoping she might emotionally and physically open up to him — or at least throw him a few scraps of validation. He was constantly met with his wife's guardedness. An awkward tension impeded intimacy and vulnerability.

Both women planted their feet firmly on the brakes of sensuality. It was difficult for them to trust not only their new husbands but themselves as well — and their inherent desires. They didn't know the path from "no" to "yes" *within themselves*.

Let's look at seven ways we can overcome such impasses.

1. When we know how arousal works for *us*, we can garner clues about how to proactively create the conditions to awaken desire and arousal in another person's mind and body. Neither man really knew what to do to change their situation. They lacked the skills to tenderly seduce their women in a way that worked for *them*. They also seemed to lack the confidence to *lead* in order to melt the resistance their wives were feeling.

2. We're not all born as master seducers. Thankfully, seduction is a skill that can be *learned*. The men were frustrated and looked defeated by their wives' responses; they'd literally shake their heads in disappointment and turn out the lights. Their wives were left in the dark feeling guilty, frustrated, and stuck in their own emotional quagmire.

3. A difference in desire often leads to a *power struggle*. This is the way sexual resistance gets set in place in relationships. A desire discrepancy quickly leads to a power struggle that ultimately undermines intimacy.

4. The lower-desire partner –the one who is feeling resistant – holds the power, even though they may prefer not to. They struggle with guilt that they're not meeting their partner's needs. They

resent feeling pressured to have sex, and they dislike feeling that every gesture of affection from their partner might only be a bid for sex. The power they hold over their partner depolarizes the relationship and ultimately undermines their mutual respect. They're in the habit of fending off sex and don't feel they have space to generate their own desire.

5. The higher-desire partner ends up feeling disempowered and resentful. They're often confused and deeply disappointed. They want their partner to initiate more; they wish to feel their partner's desire — being desired is core to their identity. They start feeling undesired and even *undesirable*. This undermines their confidence, and the emotional relationship is strained; arguments about sex erode their connection. For both partners, intimacy is lost. When they do have sex, they feel emotionally disconnected and unable to fully let go and enjoy themselves.

6. Couples may avoid discussing sex because the topic is fraught. Walls of protection keep a relationship feeling superficial. Feelings go unspoken and emotions are suppressed. When we stop sharing our intimate feelings, we feel our partner doesn't really know us or see us for who we are. When we no longer trust our partner with the deepest parts of our being, secret lives can evolve. We live in quiet desperation, or we look outside the relationship for some place or someone who might fulfill our needs. It's an age-old story we've all read in books, watched in movies, or lived out ourselves.

This is often the time when couples reach out to me for sex and relationship coaching. They sense a sexual power struggle has a stranglehold on their ability to trust and be intimate with each other. They just don't know the path forward. They'll often have seen one or more couple therapists but may have danced around the subject of sex without really getting to the root of their problem.

7. Both partners are responsible for this dynamic, and both can take action to unwind it. There's no recipe for this work. Each couple is unique. It's like putting the pieces of a puzzle together. As we work together, each piece of the puzzle is a new gesture, a new insight, a new pattern or action and, in the end, the pieces join together to reveal a new picture. One puzzle piece might be honest communication. Others could be building trust, nonsexual touch, new sexual skills, sexual polarity, intimacy building, seduction techniques, erotic explorations, and sharing of fantasies. Each piece of the puzzle connects to another until sex and intimacy is integrated as a valued part of the complete relationship picture.

I'm not suggesting that these two *Married at First Sight* couples were destined to live lives of quiet desperation or worse, but the signs were there within the first months of their marriages, and unless they changed direction, their power struggles would ultimately dictate their sexual compatibility. By the time the last episode rolled along, I was a little sad to say goodbye to the couples, and I wished them all the best, hoping they'd get the help they need to put their relationship puzzle pieces together.

56.

Sexual Confidence:
Lost and Found

Most of the clients I see in my coaching practice share a common dilemma: They lack sexual self-confidence. Life and circumstances have taken a toll on their self-confidence as lovers; without a secure foundation in that department, the staircase toward a better sex life seems daunting.

A history of sexual strife often precedes a sexless marriage or a relationship in which desires are mismatched from the start. This happens over time: each experience of silent rejection, failed initiation, or obligatory disconnected sex chips away at our confidence that we can turn on our partner or be turned on by them. It makes sense that we protect ourselves from difficult feelings, but doing so undermines the passion and connection we wish to feel with our partner. When we lose confidence in ourselves as lovers, we withdraw our enthusiasm and withhold affection. We might even create demands and confrontations.

Do you see your partner as your opponent? And sex as a negotiation? Is your partner someone against whom you must defend yourself? Such a dynamic depletes *both* partners of their sexual confidence and undermines their belief in themselves as sexually desirable and worthy lovers. If you view your partner as an opponent in the bedroom, that perspective will bleed into every other part of the relationship, wearing out your generosity and patience as well as the overall energy we bring to each other on a day-to-day basis. We may be left bewildered as to why we feel disconnected and lonely.

Acknowledging this destructive dynamic and making an agreement to put the armor of self-protection down is the first step in transforming the *battle* into an *alliance*. There are no winners in bedroom wars!

The different challenges of sexual confidence

For the masculine: Orgasm control or erection challenges can trigger a loss of confidence. Men may worry that the size of their penis is unsatisfactory for their partner. They might fret about their ability to please their partner or distrust that their sexual initiations will be welcomed.

For the feminine: Body image plays a big part in a woman's sexual confidence. If they question their attractiveness, their confidence is diminished. If they're self-conscious about their path to orgasm, their enjoyment will be inhibited. The multitasking feminine mind often finds itself easily distracted and therefore less able to fully and easily let go. This impacts women's perception of themselves as lovers with a healthy libido.

For the higher-desire partner: Confidence comes with the belief that they're desirable. If they question their desirability, their enthusiasm will be undermined, reducing sex to a disconnected bodily function rather than shared erotic enjoyment with their partner. If the higher-desire partner isn't sure their partner desires them, enjoys sex with them, or is attracted to them, then it's only natural that the ease around sexual communication and the enjoyment of sexual exploration will be dampened. If they lose confidence that their initiations are welcome, they could refrain from initiating sex altogether (in order to avoid the pain of rejection).

For the lower-desire partner: Confidence comes with knowing how arousal works in their bodies. If they often just go along with their partner's desire, they could lose confidence that their own desires matter. Sexual confidence comes with believing they're wanted for more than sex itself. When the lower-desire partner feels opened up by emotional connection and unhurried sensual seduction, they begin to connect to their own inherent desire and arousal.

Creating an environment for sexual confidence

Sexual confidence is largely an inside job; it requires that we examine the thoughts and beliefs that hold us back from expressing our authentic sexual selves. A number of processes can help unravel any unhealthy perspectives fed to us by our "inner critics." Couples in longer-term relationships can start a conversation about supporting each other's sexual self-confidence. This needs to be affirmed and nourished by experience on an ongoing basis.

When a couple works as a team, rather than as adversaries, they learn about the things that undermine each other's sexual self-confidence and potentially hold them back. We can help our partners step into their full sexual selves by speaking openly about our self-confidence and what we need to strengthen it. When we let our partners into our inner struggles, we begin to unwind our self-sabotaging beliefs and open the door for them to do the same.

57.

Mindful Touching:
For Your Own Pleasure

Three conversations with clients inspired me to write about pleasurable touch, and why many people can dish it out, but they can't take it!

The first client lamented the permanent closure of her rural massage center due to circumstances outside her control. I asked her partner if he might be able to massage her. His answer was, "Oh no, I don't know how to do that kind of thing. I'm not a big toucher."

The second is a long-time couple who I know have a wonderfully loving, Facebook-perfect relationship, yet when asked why they rarely (if ever) have sex, she honestly stated, "I don't like the way he touches me. I never have. I just don't know how to change it."

The third client told me he knows his wife loves to get massaged and caressed as part of their sexual warm-up, but he finds he can't do it for more than a few minutes without getting bored and wanting to escalate things sexually.

What to do? Well, here's a secret that every great lover knows. It's called "touching for your own pleasure." There is so much more to touch than laying our hands on another person's body. There's context, intention, expectation, desire, sensation, and communication. Touch is a language not just between you and your partner's body, but also between your hands and your brain.

Let me take you through a simple exercise to illustrate what I mean:

Step 1: Pick up a small object that fits easily into your hand. (It doesn't really matter what it is as long as it's easy to hold with two hands.)

Step 2: Take a few deep breaths, close your eyes, and start to feel the object that you're holding. Feel its shape, its edges, its contour, its weight. Pretty easy to do, right? Your brain is registering all that information.

Step 3: As you run your fingers over the object, *really slow it down*. The slower you go the more detail your brain will notice about the object. You'll find yourself noticing the *temperature* of the object, the *texture*, the *hardness* or *softness* — the smaller things you may have missed in the first round.

Step 4: Next, feel what it's like on your own skin. Is it pleasant to touch? If you run your hand over it, is there something about the object that gives you pleasure? Find the pleasure in what you're touching, even if it's just, say, its coolness on your skin, or the weight of it in your hands. Try exploring it with more than just your fingertips, perhaps with the back of your hand or between your fingers where the skin is more sensitive. Just slow down and *notice*. You'll see that slowing down heightens your awareness and awakens your curiosity.

You've just brought *mindfulness* to your touch. You've made the space and taken the time to go deeper into your experience and expand it to include what is already present but previously unnoticed. Mindful touch separates the great lovers from the mediocre, the passionate from the uninspired.

Why start with an inanimate object? Because we have *no obligation* to make the object feel good! We're not trying to win the object's approval. The object has no preferences or expectations for us to meet. Touching an inanimate object is purely about our own experience.

When was the last time you sat down to pet a cat? We pet a cat to offer them pleasure, but we're also drawn to touch the soft fur and feel it run between our fingers. We enjoy the warmth and silkiness against our hands. So, on one level we pet the cat for our own pleasure. Likewise, when we learn how to touch for our own pleasure, our lover feels the difference. Things slow down; touch becomes varied rather than repetitive, and sensation is heightened through mutual awareness. We pay attention to the experience of both *giving* and *receiving*.

Through mindfulness we draw out the pleasure of the moment. We're fed by the gift we give, which creates a circuit of enjoyment felt by giver and receiver alike. Consider *what you want to communicate* before you touch someone. And choose the form of *touch language* that matches your communication. If your partner needs to feel comforted, you may be tender, and touch gently to soothe and nurture. You might cradle or rock them in your arms or place their head on your lap and softly stroke their hair.

If you feel romantic, you might touch your partner's cheek softly with the back of your hand, trace their lips with the tip of your finger, or run your hand along the contour of their body. If you feel passion rising, your touch might become more assertive; you might hold their wrists above their head. This could lead to gentle biting, light scratching, tugging their hair, and pressing up against them, body to body. You could confidently hold, grab, and squeeze as you pull them close to you. If you both feel playful, you might try spanking, tickling, or wrestling.

Another secret every great lover knows is that *touching doesn't have to lead to sex*. Give yourselves both a break from stressful strategies and unmet expectations. When you separate sex from touch, you create an opportunity to be with what's happening, which is sometimes *touch for its own sake*. By removing the destination, we're left to enjoy the journey – to be in the moment!

Share this chapter with your lover and decide who will be the giver and receiver. Set aside 30 minutes to explore touch from this perspective, with no other agenda. Enjoy your explorations in giving touch by including your own pleasure in every moment of intimate contact. Enjoy the mystery of your partner's body from a place of openness, curiosity, and wonderment!

58.

Touch:
Love in Action

The etiquette of the COVID period presented many of us with unique challenges. One time I was helping a friend celebrate his birthday with three other people at a little outdoor soirée where mask-wearing and social distancing were in effect. When someone held up a camera to take a picture of the birthday boy, I jumped up and — without thinking — wrapped my arm around him and snuggled up close for the camera. In that split second, I completely forgot that touching was frowned upon at that time.

I lurched back, apologizing for my momentary lapse.

"When was the last time someone touched you?" I asked.

"It's been six months!" he answered, shocked at his own words.

Due to COVID, something as natural as touching a friend in a happy moment had been taken away from us.

My hairdresser later remarked at how many people told her she was the first person to touch them in six months. When she asked about the last time they were hugged, they could all recount the time and place in detail.

A simple touch, a pat, or a hand on the shoulder triggers instantaneous changes in our bodies. Our brains produce oxytocin. Studies show this chemical makes us feel more generous, empathetic, nurturing, collaborative, and *grateful*. Gratitude stimulates the release of other feel-good hormones such as *dopamine* and *serotonin* while it reduces stress hormones such as *cortisol* and *norepinephrine*. These neurochemical changes make us feel happier and less stressed. We now understand through science that physical touch can lessen depression and anxiety, boost our immune systems, and even relieve pain!

It's not surprising, then, that I've noticed how gratitude is present in my life more than ever, not just because of bonding hormones, but because I now see that something as natural as reaching out and touching someone *can be taken from me*. When I lie in bed with my partner these days, I snuggle up close to his warm body. I'm more aware of the privilege of being close to someone. I stop for hugs more often, and I let them linger. I feel the goodness flow through my brain and nervous system. The trauma of a pandemic has given me a deeper appreciation of any physical contact. Holding hands, massaging shoulders, TV cuddling — I'm more aware of it all. In place of these being entitlements, they feel more like blessings! In fact, *they are!*

Couples can find themselves in the same predicament as their single friends. It's not uncommon for long-term partners to let nonsexual touching fall by the wayside. They sit in separate chairs to watch TV together. They go to bed at different times. They hold their kid's hands rather than their partner's. Even touches of comfort or condolence become awkward. Is it surprising then that intimacy suffers if touch is only given as a bid for sex?

If you're in a domestic relationship, think of all the touch experiences you can add to life with your partner. Rather than the occasional side shoulder hug or pat on the back, here are some new ways we can invite touch into our day-to-day lives:

Extended hugging: At least once a day, hug someone for 20 seconds. (It doesn't sound long until you do it!) It takes 20 seconds for your hormones to really kick in with the oxytocin, so "let go" into the hug. Start to take a few deep breaths together and just hold on in a relaxed way. When one of you initiates the release, separate and say *thank you*. Your brain chemicals will do the rest.

Facials: Every woman (and many men) knows what it's like to get a facial. Pull out the facial creams from the back of your closet or, even better, learn to make your own with ingredients like honey, milk, oatmeal, and steam. We all loved to be pampered, and Lord knows we can use it!

Sensual wrestling: Touching doesn't always have to come in a tender, loving form. It can come with playful tension, pressing, pulling, and pushing. Moving energy is important when we're stressed and feeling disconnected from our partners. I suggest you make agreements about *boundaries* (for instance to protect sore shoulders or tender knees). Keep in mind that bigger bodies can easily overpower! With agreements in place, get down on the carpet and let loose!

Dancing: When was the last time you set aside fifteen minutes to put on the tunes from your teens and dance your heart out? Not knowing how to dance is no excuse! You know each other well enough to lose face with awkward dance moves. Hold on to each other, laugh, and let the music move you.

Partner yoga: Leaning into another body for support and stretching can feel *so good!* Slow, conscious movement together creates trust. Just like sensual wrestling, we can play with the polarity of leading and following. (*Search online for "partner yoga for beginners" for ideas.*)

Sensation meditation: For fun, take turns giving each other unusual sensory experiences using different objects, from soft to scratchy or from hot to cold, for example. Blindfold the recipient so they don't know what to expect. Wake up each other's skin receptors and invite them out to play!

Massage: If you don't already own one, buy a massage table and treat each other to weekly full-body sensual massage. Rather than a bed where massage can morph into a few minutes of sexual foreplay, a massage table sets the scene for an extended touch experience, where partners take turns giving and receiving. You don't need to go to massage school to send your partner into sensory bliss! (*Search online for "couples massage for beginners" and let your fingers do the talking.*)

Shower/bathe together: If you have the space to both get under some running water, take turns soaping each other down. Let your partner shampoo your hair and wash your body. Let go of control for a while and be a baby again (right down to the towel drying).

Get creative. Don't treat this list as complete. Instead, discuss more ways to touch each other! Every couple is different, and there's no gold standard for touching. Make it part of your relationship conversation, knowing it's an important part of staying intimately connected. Whether you're partnered or single, find ways to give and receive touch. Whether you ask for it or pay for it, give your body what it naturally needs to stay balanced, calm, and connected!

59.

Becoming Bob:
The Shameless Art of Loving Vulvas

When I first saw Eve Ensler's *The Vagina Monologues* in 1996, one of the monologues stood out to me. It was a woman's account of being intimate with a man named Bob. This is some of what she wrote:

"...Turned out that Bob loved vaginas. He was a connoisseur. He loved the way they felt, the way they tasted, the way they smelled, but most importantly he loved the way they looked. He had to look at them. The first time we had sex, he told me he had to see me..."

Becoming a 'Bob' is a journey of discovery any heterosexual man can take. It begins with honoring the vulva (a more accurate word to describe the totality of a woman's genitals) and the woman to whom it belongs. In Ensler's account, Bob's perspective on female genitalia helped heal her of her own shame and self-consciousness, and in so doing, opened her to embrace self-acceptance of her body and her pleasure.

"...I hated my thighs, and I hated my vagina even more. I thought it was incredibly ugly. I was one of those women who had looked at it and from that moment on I wished I hadn't. It made me sick. I pitied anyone who had to go down there..."

On one hand women get messages about loving our bodies while at the same time we read about the latest nip and tuck procedures like "designer vulva" surgery. We're left believing that the look of our vulva is just one more thing women need to feel insecure about. But the truth is women don't have to pay someone to "fix" us so we can look more *normal*.

Rather than give our money to doctors or hide ourselves from our partners, we can redirect the cultural tide away from shame to embrace self-acceptance, appreciation and diversity. I coach women from every walk of life – age group, race, ethnicity, income level, political grouping, and sexual orientation. A vast number of these women tell me they don't feel altogether comfortable with their genitals. In a survey of over 3,000 women, almost half said they had concerns about the appearance of their vulvas that left them feeling self-conscious.

A surprising number of my female clients have never (or rarely) taken a mirror and looked at themselves "down there". Unlike men, we can't easily see ourselves the way our partner sees us. Unless we're in bed with a "Bob," a partner who's not shy about their adoration, we don't get a lot of feedback about what a partner thinks about our genitals.

"This is awfully intimate," I said. "Can't we just do it?"

"No," he said. "It's who you are. I need to look."

"I held my breath. He looked and looked. He got breathy and his face changed. He didn't look ordinary anymore. He looked like a hungry beast."

"You're so beautiful," he said. "You're elegant and deep and innocent and wild."

"You saw that there?" I said.

It was like he read my palm. "I saw that," he said, "and more — much, much more."

When a woman feels safe and confident enough to open her legs for her lover, she gives them permission to take in her natural beauty. When she can see the look of awe on her lover's face as they gaze at her feminine softness, and when she can unselfconsciously hear their words of appreciation and adoration, describing to her what they see, she crosses a threshold into her own sexual empowerment.

It's a rite of passage that marks a turning point in every woman's sexual confidence and awakening.

"He stayed looking for almost an hour as if he were studying a map, observing the moon, staring into my eyes, but it was my vagina. In the light I watched him looking at me and he was so genuinely excited, so peaceful and euphoric, I began to get wet and turned on."

We all long for our lovers to adore our bodies, to drink us in like a fine wine and savor every inch of us. An adoring lover teaches us how to love ourselves. They hold the mirror of adoration up for us so we can see our own beauty through their eyes. The truth is, every woman's vulva is completely unique and aesthetically perfect just as it is, just like our face or eyes or any other part of us. As Bob says, "it's who you are".

The beauty of the vulva is reflected everywhere in nature – flowers, fruit, a mountain crevasse. Artists and photographers capture these sensually delicate forms, and poets have praised and adored the female form for millennia. The natural elegance of the female genitalia captures the heart of every awakened lover.

"I began to see myself the way he saw me. I began to feel beautiful and delicious — like a great painting, or a waterfall. Bob wasn't afraid. He wasn't grossed out. I began to swell, began to feel proud. Began

to love my vagina. And Bob, lost himself there, and I was there with him, in my vagina, and we were gone."

If you've never seen Eve Ensler performing Vagina Monologues, I recommend you look it up on YouTube. It was brave in 1996, and it still is.

My wish is that every woman at some point in life meets a "Bob" (male or female) to help open her to her own unique feminine beauty. And my wish for every lover of women is that they learn how to become a "Bob" devoted to worshiping nature's Goddess-like perfection.

60.

Consent:
Putting the Sexy into Consent

What does consent mean in long-term relationships? One of my couple clients came to me to discuss the fallout of a "nonconsensual" incident that resulted in one of them feeling angry and the other confused. The man made the mistake of not asking his partner's consent to try out something new in the bedroom. Rather than talking about it with her beforehand, he showed up in the bedroom with handcuffs and proceeded to lock her arms behind her back. There was no prior conversation about using restraints and no mutual exploration on the subject of bondage beforehand. In effect, consent was not given, and because of that things didn't go well. At all.

Sexual consent was not born out of the MeToo movement. Sexual consent is actually one of the defining terms of our era. It first appeared as a slow, percolating drip over the last few decades, starting out in more fringe sexual communities like kink, where consent conversations are taught and expected. The LGBTQ community also laid down the tracks of open consent conversations when it comes to sex. Sexual consent kept people feeling safe and understood in their desires and expectations.

Once society started confronting consent breaches in the public forum and social media, the floodgates gushed open. Sexual consent became a household conversation. The MeToo movement will go down in history as the nozzle to that floodgate. It challenges power structures and educates us on the importance of clear conversations when it comes to our desires and our bodies. Consent

- undermines power structures;
- gives a voice to all parties;
- creates sexual equality and safety;
- clarifies sexual expectations and reduces rejection; and
- helps all parties to get their needs met.

The internet is full of advice on how to have a consent conversation with a new partner, and why it's imperative to represent your wishes and boundaries, especially when it comes to intimacy with someone you don't know well. In the case of long-term relationships, consent is a multi-layered consideration. It's less black and white. It's not simply a "yes" or "no" question. It's more nuanced because in long-term relationships, consent is often *implied*.

What is implied consent?

Communication about sex, in and of itself, is limited in most relationships, so sexual initiation is often short-handed into an exchange of a certain look, a caress, or an innuendo. Partners come to believe they know each other well enough that conversations about desires, requests, or agreements aren't necessary. They know the pattern, the time of day, and the moves that bring them together for sex. In some relationships this is fine, but couples might bypass deeper conversations and slip into assumptions about sexual routines that are familiar, by virtue of the couple's sexual history. Consent is implied. We're not going to press charges against our partner if they squeeze our butt in the kitchen, are we? If we pull our partner close to us in bed with sexual desire, consent is implied. Couples know each other's cues — verbal and nonverbal — that reliably guide them into sexual play together.

Conversely, we also know the signs when our partner isn't *interested* in sex. We can feel it in their bodies, their words, and their gestures. Couples come to read consent in all sorts of ways that don't necessarily require a sit-down conversation. But familiarity can be a double-edged sword when it comes to consent. When we stop talking about intimacy, we begin to form expectations and make presumptions about our partner's needs and desires. This can lead to misunderstandings and rejection. It happens all the time. This is why I teach couples about consent and why it's important in long-term relationships.

Furthermore, our sexual tastes can change over time. What once worked for us might not serve us anymore. We might think we know what our partner likes sexually, but unless we become comfortable talking about sex, we can't be certain. Think about it: How many partners are agreeing to sexual acts to keep the peace or avoid an uncomfortable conversation? If pleasing our partner becomes a primary motive for having sex, we might get used to bypassing our own desires.

In long-term relationships, consent means more than just asking for sex; it's asking about what *kind* of sex we want. Again, it's not a simple "yes" or "no" question. It's a *conversation* about needs and desires. It's *checking in* with your partner and ensuring that you both have an opportunity to express an enthusiastic "yes" to what's being offered, whether that's a foot massage, intercourse, or something new on the erotic menu.

Knowing what you want sexually

When the initiating partner starts to include "consent" conversations in their sexual relationship, they increase their chances of not being rejected. Why? Because they begin asking open-ended questions that lead with curiosity about their partner's desires and needs. By asking open-ended questions, they make it possible for their partner's "no" to turn into a "maybe" or even a "yes." They might discover one night that their partner's "no" to sexual intercourse doesn't preclude them giving and receiving oral sex, reaching orgasms in other ways, enjoying something more playful, or simply sharing intimacy that doesn't lead to orgasm. By expanding consent beyond a "yes" or "no" answer, it's all on the table to be discussed.

When we ask what our partner is up for sexually, we give them a chance to reflect on their own desire in the moment. This is (surprisingly) something that couples stop doing. Sexual consent is about inviting our partner to feel their desires in the moment by taking the time to ask them. Here are some possible approaches:

- "How are you feeling tonight?"
- "I'd love to share some intimate time together.
- "Would you like to set aside some time for that?"
- "Let's talk about what that might look like."
- "Do you have any desires you'd like to share with me?"
- "Let's talk about what would make you feel good right now."

Let's get clear that disappointment is a natural part of consent conversations. No matter how much awareness we bring to consent and initiation, there will be times when our partner won't meet our needs. It's important to deal with moments of disappointment without falling into blame, shame, feelings of rejection, or emotional withdrawal. If we subtly or overtly punish our partner for not giving their sexual consent to something, we're creating an environment where honest feelings can't be heard and accepted.

When we are able to experience disappointment without blaming our partner, we keep the doors of communication open. When we allow for our partner's honest answers, without getting moody and pulling away, we let our partner know that their sexual consent is important to us.

It's worth mentioning that if sexual trauma is part of your or your partner's past, consent conversations can be opportunities to heal old wounds and reestablish trust.

Unlearning bad sex education

We're not taught about consent conversations in mainstream entertainment. Usually, sex happens without many words. We're shown that sex sweeps both willing partners up in a passionate embrace that ends with sexual intercourse and mutual, simutaneous orgasms.

This might work well in Hollywood films, but this kind of wordless approach to sex isn't sustainable in long-term relationships. If a couple hopes to enjoy a vibrant, growing sex life throughout their journey together, then open honest conversations about desires and consent is imperative. Consent conversations acknowledge that we're not always the same in our desires from week to week or even day to day.

It might sound strange, but consent is actually *sexy*. People in those aforementioned kink and BDSM communities often discover this. Imagine, consciously negotiating what will happen behind closed doors! Being authentic and saying what you really want! Perhaps taking a risk and — to your surprise — the other party saying "Yes!"

I have no doubt that the next generation will inhabit a very different sexual world. They already have little patience for sexual bigotry when it comes to gender, sexual preferences, and identity. They're far more accepting of those who are different from them, and their sexual openness is less complicated by shame and puritanism. I hope they'll continue to live in a world where consent is a sexy conversation of possibilities and nonconsensual sex will be looked upon as old-fashioned and uptight.

Talking about sex takes courage. Sometimes it's even harder to talk about sex with a long-term partner. It's easy to "let it slide" and fall back on familiarity and routine. So let me be the voice in your ear encouraging you to start having those consent conversations in your relationship. You might be surprised where it leads.

61.

Sex Toys:
Are They Bridging the "Orgasm Gap"?

If you opened the drawer of 53 percent of women's bedside tables, you'd find a vibrator or two. We've finally reached a tipping point that makes owning a sex toy pretty normal.

Thank goodness!

According to data released last year, sex toys are a $15 billion industry, making them more mainstream than ever. Today, women's pleasure is now a primary focus of the sex toy industry, and vibrators for solo and partner sex is a big part of women's pleasure.

Sexual accessories like masturbation toys are a shame-free part of a healthy woman's private sex life. Yet, according to studies, many of these women who enjoy their private time with their vibrators are hesitant to "invite their toys to the party" when they have sex with their partner.

I coach people of all ages and cultures who've expressed reluctance to include sex toys in their intimate time with a partner. They either suspect (or have been told) that their partner is worried a good vibrator will replace them in the bedroom. I've heard this point of view for decades now and I have to say, *it's getting a little old*. We need to have an honest and open conversation about what sex toys offer (and don't offer) the women who own them.

Hello science!

A few years ago, researcher Laurie Mintz identified heterosexual women as the group least sexually satisfied when it came to sex. According to recent studies by the Kinsey Institute, 80 percent of women from ages 18 to 94 report they cannot reach orgasm through intercourse alone and need some other form of stimulation. (Compare this to 94 percent of men who say they *do* reach orgasm from intercourse.) This is referred to as the "Orgasm Gap" and when these statistics hit the news, pretty much every media outlet and magazine was talking about it.

Sadly, only in *the last twenty years* has the clitoris been acknowledged for the role it plays in a woman's orgasmic satisfaction. Isn't that incredible? Until recently, very little was known about female sexual arousal and a woman's path to orgasm. Dating back to the 15th century, research on female sexuality has been ignored, suppressed, and dismissed as unworthy of scientific study.

Mintz argues that the primary reason for this form of gender inequality stems from "our cultural ignorance of the clitoris" and that it is commonplace to "mislabel women's genitals by the one part (the vagina) that gives men, but not women, reliable orgasms." Research explains what women have always known: the vaginal canal is designed for insemination and birthing. In and of itself, it's not where women find their most orgasmic pleasure — at least, not on its own.

With the advent of MRI technology, we've come to understand that the clitoris is a much larger organ than was previously understood. What we call the "clit" is just the visible part of an organ that goes much further beneath the skin's surface and plays a much larger role in a woman's orgasmic capacity than the vagina.

The clitoris has 8,000 sensitive nerve endings (double the amount of a penis). Its internal structure has arms that extend down from the visible nub, wrapping around the vaginal opening. It also reaches back into a woman's G-Spot area, just inside the vagina. The entire clitoral structure contributes to both external and internal orgasms. One of the more interesting acknowledgments from the scientific community is that the clitoris is unique in that its sole purpose is sexual pleasure. It's the only human organ dedicated to arousal.

Women's sexual pleasure, and how it actually works, has finally taken its rightful place in the world of scientific study. Men are welcome to come along for the ride, if they're willing to adapt to what we now know about enhancing their female partner's orgasmic experience. (Keep in mind that studies of the female orgasm and clitoral research are still news to most people. It's unfolding before our eyes as science gets its head out of the sand and finally turns its attention to female sexuality and arousal.)

Implications for sex toys

As is often the case, profit opportunities are never far behind cultural shifts and trends. We now have a female-centric industry of sex toys designed to optimize women's sexual pleasure, many of which are focused on the female orgasm (inside and outside), using the latest vibration technology. Walk into any well-provisioned sex shop and you'll find entire walls displaying dozens of different makes and models, as well as educated sale clerks who are very used to answering the most intimate questions.

Sex toys are playing a primary role in the evolution of female sexuality and (in my opinion) can play an important part in a couple's sex life.

(Therapists of yesteryear didn't refer to them as "marital aids" for no reason!)

A cornerstone of a great sex life is communication. Discussing sex toys with your partner opens the door to sharing desires and asking for what you want. The more you can talk about these things together, the more likely your sex life with your partner will be active, honest, and enjoyable!

When a couple initiates a conversation about sex toys, they are

- making sex and intimacy a natural topic of conversation (Yay!);
- acknowledging that sexual pleasure matters for both partners;
- agreeing to explore as a team, and open their minds to new ways of giving and receiving pleasure;
- actively bringing variety and novelty into their sex life; and
- committing to a life of pleasure and play together.

If an initial vibrator turns out to be a gateway to other sex toys, so be it! Scroll through an online store to learn about what's new on the market or visit one of the many women-friendly sex toy stores, now commonly found in most urban centers. It's a fun and exciting adventure for a couple. Every year, new designs, new technology, and new materials offer couples new orgasmic experiences. (You know couples are breaking out the toys together just by watching the new designs for couple's vibrators hitting the market. Vibration, as a pathway to arousal, is not going away.)

Heterosexual men, please rest assured that you will not be replaced by a vibrator! A vibrator won't seduce your partner. It can't whisper in her ear. It doesn't have a warm body to press up against or hold in the afterglow. When it comes to a blood-pumping, energy-flowing, pheromone-charged experience, nothing beats the real deal! When you welcome toys into your sex life, you're supporting your partner's connection with their own body and their own orgasmic pleasure.

Ask your female partner to pull out her favorite toy from her bedside drawer and show you how she likes to use it. Learn how to use it on each other. Explore each other's many erogenous zones. You may discover your own vibrational pleasures. Some vibrators are designed specifically for the male body.

By closing the Orgasm Gap in your relationship (however you do it), your female partner will suddenly become a lot more interested in planning your next party. *Trust me.*

62.

You Be You:
Are You Being Sexually Authentic?

A client shared with me that the reason she doesn't want to show her partner the new kinky sex toys she ordered is because he might make her feel silly. She assumed he wouldn't share her desires and was too afraid to ask. Another time, a client confided that he wanted to take his partner to a "clothing optional" resort in California. I asked him why he hadn't done that.

"She'd never do something like that," he replied.

"How do you know if you don't ask her?" I said.

"I just know," was his answer.

Another of my clients is a woman who had never experienced an orgasm until we did some work together. She'd longed to become orgasmic. However, up until then she'd chosen to fake her orgasms with her partner for fear of how it might impact their sex life. Even though she can now orgasm on her own, she remained too shy to orgasm with her partner, and the deception continued.

I have another client who loves to cross-dress. He's not the first (and likely won't be the last) cross-dressing client I've coached. Because of the stigma attached to this particular fetish, most crossdressers remain closeted from their partners for fear of rejection.

We all have inner stories that inhibit us from fully sharing our erotic desires and our authentic selves with sexual partners. Even though the clients I just mentioned can't yet be sexually authentic with their partners, they're able to share their true feelings in coaching sessions. They find self-acceptance in the confidentiality of those sessions.

This provides a significant clue about the first step on your journey toward sexual authenticity. We all make choices as to what we share with others and what we don't share. Real consequences can attend the telling of a difficult truth. Are we willing to pay the price that may come with speaking up? That depends on the situation. If your partner buys a new shirt that doesn't look especially good on them (in your opinion) not much rides on telling them the truth. But if you don't enjoy sex with your partner because of the way they touch you, or your desires aren't being met, then telling the truth has a greater risk (and a greater possible reward).

Honesty about sex allows us to communicate what works for us sexually and why. The number one reason most people say they don't speak their truth to their partner is because they don't want to hurt their feelings. But I think it runs deeper than that. I believe we don't speak our truth because we're not confident about having a conversation that will lead us to deeper intimacy. Conversations about sex and what we desire create risk — risk that we'll be judged, shamed, or that we'll lose the love of our partner. This is a risk many of us aren't willing to take!

The alternative to sexual honesty is the denial of our desires, going along with sex that doesn't work for us or worse, being in a relationship with no sex at all! The alternative to sexual honesty is we end up living sexually inauthentic lives, and we pay a big price for it. The *price* is that we never discover what's on the other side of honest conversations. We form stories about our partner's ability to hear our truth, to justify our silence. Sexual silence is laden with tension; the unspoken conversations can weigh heavily on our relationships both in and out of the bedroom.

Consider this. Your partner may not only be willing to *hear* what you have to share; they might *welcome* it! They might be withholding their own truth for the same reasons! For all you know, you might both be living sexually inauthentic lives with each other.

If you feel this is true for you and your partner, it's time to break the silence. Truth will lead you to your next steps, whatever they may be. And most importantly, you'll feel the freedom of living a sexually authentic life.

63.

Who are you, really?

In my experience of talking to couples, I have found most have not explored the answer to this question when it comes to their erotic life.

I invite you to become a beginner again by exploring new forms of intimacy and erotic expression. I encourage you to engage in conversations that help you grow as a couple and help you become increasingly comfortable in your sexuality, whatever flavor it happens to be. Sexual empowerment means learning *who you are sexually* and teaching your partner *how to love you* the *way you want* to be loved.

Note that our desires can change over time. Couples in long-term love can shift and grow in their paths to arousal or turn-on. There's no right or wrong way to express your eroticism as an individual or a couple. What works for some doesn't work for others. In the world of healthy sexuality, we learn to leave our judgments at the door! The more you learn about the fascinating world of human sexuality, the more at ease you'll be with your own explorations.

"Who am I?"

This question is probably most urgent in our teens and twenties as we develop our identity in the world. We have a deep need to belong, find our place in community, and join with others who accept us. Our sexuality is a big part of that exploration, with pressures coming from all directions to conform to a sexual identity that is both socially acceptable within our tribe and true to who we know ourselves to be on the inside. If we're lucky we can experience both.

However, our sexual explorations often end once we think we've found our answer, and that can happen *far too soon!* Social norms, bad sex education, expectations from lovers — even our own resignation and frustration — can halt our sexual explorations and fulfillment. We end up seeing our sexuality through the narrow lens of what life has given us, either in our lack of exposure, our partner's preferences, or our own perspective of what's "right or wrong." Too often, couples find themselves settling into a sexual routine that dulls their enthusiasm and stunts their growth. "My partner and I aren't sexually matched," is a common refrain.

What Do I Want to Feel?

The variety of erotic inclinations became apparent to me in my early years of coaching. Couples would describe their desires with phrases like, "I want my partner to be more assertive. I want them to take me." or "I wish my partner would slow down, look into my eyes, and tell me that they love me." or "I love it when my partner brings toys like blindfolds into the bedroom. I get aroused when they tie my hands down."

There are multiple paths to arousal, and they each have a *feeling* attached to them. The *feeling* we're looking for during sex will influence the sexual flavor we're most attracted to. By getting curious and asking our partner the right questions we can learn what feelings they want to experience during sex. *Your Erotic Menu* will help you have these enlightening conversations that will serve to deepen your erotic connection as a couple.

64.

A Banquet of Flavors

Sexuality is so much more than what most of us have been taught, or grown up to expect. It's not done in one way that's considered *normal*. It's not gender specific or older-age restricted. It's not a performance. It doesn't even have to include other people. Sexuality comes in a rainbow of energies and a banquet of flavors.

Sex can invite us to be light and playful, and it can be intense and psychological. Sex can open our hearts to romance, or unite us in sacred union. Sex can heal us of our pain, and introduce us to new-found pleasures. Sex can lead us into the deeper and more shadowy feelings that lie under the surface, waiting to be revealed.

Sexual energy is the human birth-right that we all have in common. How we express our sexual energy and experience it is our choice based on who we are erotically, our life experiences, and our own sexual self-awareness.

Learning about the full-spectrum of sexual expressions informs that self-awareness, which is why I created Your Erotic Menu.

When I assembled a checklist of erotic activities, it made the most sense to group them into six erotic flavors/styles to help clients understand the full-spectrum of experiences available to explore. They are Sensual, Romantic, Tantric, Passionate, Fetish and Kinky.

When I ask clients to check off activities that appeal to them, most will lean toward the flavor/style that is familiar to them. But often what is most familiar is not where transformation lies.

We're all capable of stepping into multiple sides of our erotic selves. I believe all six erotic flavors live within every one of us. Some flavors are more familiar to us than others, and some rarely see the light of day.

Shining some light on our more unexplored erotic flavors/styles opens doors to new awareness within ourselves, as well as new dynamics with our partner.

My job/passion/calling, as a sex coach, is to re-educate clients and expand their experience of sex.

Sexual satisfaction is what everyone strives for, but without reexamining our sexuality and embarking on explorations that lie outside of our current sexual expression, we still face obstacles to our sexual fulfillment. Our biggest obstacles are the self-imposed limits that keep us safe inside our familiar boxes. Outside of these boxes lies curiosity, open-mindedness and new sides of our erotic selves.

What does sexual satisfaction mean to you? Here are some of the prerequisites that most of my clients would agree constitute a fulfilling sex life in a relationship:

- Passion and erotic excitement
- Intimacy and connection
- Authentic sexual expression
- Novelty, variety and curiosity
- Emotional safety and integrity

Each of these sexual attributes can be found in all six sexual flavors.

We are all multi-dimensional in our sexuality. When both partners begin to explore their erotic minds, share their fantasies and curiosities, they come to see themselves and each other in a new light.

If you've been a sensualist all your life, consider exploring different erotic energies like passion or kink. If sex has always been a high energy lustful event, romance or tantra may make you a more versatile lover to your partner.

When partners give themselves and each other permission to explore, they open themselves to new discoveries that often heighten their sexual polarity and transform their experience as a couple.

When a couple says YES to exploring, they're saying...

YES to revealing more of their erotic selves,

YES to being a beginner again and learning new things together,

YES to discovering what's authentic in their sexual expression, and

YES to asking for what they want from their partner to support that expression.

I created *Your Erotic Menu* to help couples in their exploration of what is true to them. It starts with an extensive checklist of erotic activities that cover six erotic flavors. In this online course I guide couples in expanding their erotic menus in a way that is sensitive, knowledgeable, and shame-free.

Your Erotic Menu is just the beginning of many open and honest conversations about sex. Many of my clients have told me they wish they'd received this *adult sex education* decades ago. *Your Erotic Menu* online course is my gift to you. You'll find your exclusive access link to the course in Your Next Steps at the end of this book.

65.

Your Erotic Menu:
A Communication Exercise for Curious Couples

Most people will understand an *erotic menu* to mean the activities they engage in during sex. But if I ask a client what's on their erotic menu, they'll often look perplexed. They'll start with kissing, touching, oral sex and intercourse but, after these more obvious activities, they realize their list is actually pretty short.

"I mean, how many things can two people do during sex?" was what a client asked me once.

I decided to answer that question quite literally. So, I created a very long, full-spectrum list of sexual activities that range from sensual, to tantric, to romantic, to passionate, to fetish, to kink. I called it *Your Erotic Menu* and put it online as a course for couples who want to grow their menu.

It teaches couples how to talk about sex with curiosity and honesty. It also introduces new ideas to add to your erotic menu from a list of activities that appeal to a large cross- section of lovers.

It's universally acknowledged amoung the most respected sex therapists that one of the antidotes to sexual boredom is novelty. Novelty shifts our state; it engages our brain and arousal system in new ways; it also lifts the veil of familiarity and routine so we can see our partner in a new light and with a new erotic perspective. Novelty realigns our attraction to our partner and reintroduces sexual polarity back into our dynamic.

Here are some other well-recognized strategies to enliven sexual desire.

- Introducing adventure, like learning something new, and trying new things together.
- Expanding your awareness of human sexuality in its vast array of tastes and preferences.
- Coming together as a team, and proactively taking steps to improve your sex life.
- Starting to talk about sex in a way that is curious, interested, and inviting.

After I compiled this very long list of full-spectrum erotic activities I knew I couldn't just give it to clients without making sure they knew how to use the list to actually bring about change in their sex lives.

I wanted to support couples in using the checklist to actually transform how they talk about sex. By getting curious, communicating their desires, and sharing their fantasies, couples learn how to feel safe to share what so often is left unspoken.

By identifying activities that excite or engage our imagination, and then sharing our interests with our partner, we open the door to conversations that inspire us to grow and explore beyond what is overly familiar and comfortably routine.

We begin to see sex as a journey with many roads to explore along the way, rather than just a *7.5 minute* end-of-the-day stress release. It is a journey of exploration and continuous learning that actually has no endpoint.

It's fascinating to read through a list of multi-flavored erotic activities. When we're exposed to this kind of sexual diversity, we can't help but become more tolerant and less judgemental of tastes that fall outside of our range of interest. Together we make a diverse and beautiful banquet of human sexual expressions that lie outside of concepts like *right or wrong*.

As I often say, we are no more responsible for what turns us on than we are for the color of our eyes. Self-acceptance, acceptance of others, curiosity and consent are all part of being a sex-positive grown-up. There is no *normal* in sexuality, therefore there's no standard to which we should hold ourselves or others.

Sex can be psychological, physical, deep, and playful. It can be romantic. It can challenge our limits, and it can open our hearts.

Sex is whatever you want it to be. How you and your partner agree to engage in sex is up to both of you and the guidelines you have agreed upon.

Talking about sex with a curious mind and authentic desire is the first step in deciding the kind of sex you want and the role it will play in your life.

I'm looking forward to hearing how this erotic communication exercise works for you. Whether you're dating or in a long-term relationship, talking about your sexual desires with your partner is key to being a great lover.

Enjoy this online erotic communication course. Stretch it out over a few sittings. I have a feeling your list will be too long to fit into one evening. *Your Erotic Menu* online course is my gift to you. You'll find your exclusive access link to the course in Your Next Steps at the end of this book.

Don't Stop Now!

I hope this book has opened new conversations, new doors of experience, and deepened your understanding of yourself and your partner when it comes to your emotional and erotic life together.

We've touched on every aspect, every challenge, and every lesson that a turned-on couple encounters in their life together.

Part 1: Tune In – You learned the essential skills for building a secure and loving foundation for your intimacy to thrive.

Part 2: Turn Up – You delved into the mysterious world of desire, discovering how to express and amplify your desires with confidence and authenticity.

Part 3: Turn On – You embarked on a voyage of sexual exploration as a way to cultivate a deeply satisfying and fulfilling erotic connection.

If there's one thing I want you to take away from reading this book, it's that there is no *normal* you need to compare yourself to when it comes to sex and intimacy.

There's no *normal* sexual frequency, no *normal* way to express your sexuality. Your desires are uniquely yours to discover yourself and share with your partner. What brings most couples to my virtual door is the discrepancy that leads to hurt feelings, loss of honest conversations, and a sincere desire to find their common ground.

As a coach, my desired outcome in working with clients is that they develop the trust to talk honestly about sex, discover what is authentic to them as individuals, and confidently ask for what they want from each other.

I encourage you to not stop here. I'm leaving you with next steps so that what you've learned about your intimacy, desires, and preferred sexual style can be integrated into your relationship. Below I introduce you to *Your Erotic Menu* to keep your passion and connection alive and ever growing.

Your Next Step:

Your Erotic Menu (the online course)

Now, it's time to take your intimacy to the next level. I created this immersive online course as a tool to facilitate new ways of talking about sex with your partner.

Your Erotic Menu is a communication exercise. It's an adult couple's game. It's a coaching process. It's sex-ed for grownups.

What Your Erotic Menu Offers You:

- **Rediscover each other:** Whether you've been together for years or just started dating, this exercise is your chance to see your partner with fresh eyes.

- **Learn about your partner's erotic mind:** When you understand each other's paths to arousal you'll both grow in your confidence to please your partner.

- **Expand your erotic horizons:** Learn to express your deepest desires, share your curiosities, and communicate your boundaries. This full-spectrum list of erotic activities will guide you in adding novelty and excitement to your sex life.

- **Build a foundation of openness:** During this course you will uncover more about each other than many couples do in a lifetime. It will set the tone for an open, honest, and consensual sexual relationship that will enrich every aspect of your life together.

- **Learn about six unique flavors or styles of sexual expression:** Embark on an erotic adventure as you explore sensual, romantic, tantric, passionate, fetish, and kink.

What You'll Learn:

- **Discover new desires:** Expand your erotic menu and uncover new interests.

- **Enhance your communication skills:** Learn to talk openly and honestly about sex.

- **Create novelty and variety:** Introduce new elements to your sex life to keep it exciting, playful and fulfilling.

- **Deep dive into a full-spectrum exploration of six erotic flavors.** Discover the vast world of human sexuality.

Why It's Important to Talk About Sex:

- **Express Your Deepest Desires:** Many couples struggle to talk about their sexual needs and fantasies, which can lead to dissatisfaction and a feeling of being unfulfilled. *Your Erotic Menu* provides a safe and structured way to express these desires, ensuring both partners feel heard and valued.

- **Share Your Curiosities:** Curiosity is a natural and healthy part of a sexual relationship – but without open communication, it can remain unexplored. This course encourages you to share your curiosities, fostering a sense of adventure and mutual discovery.

- **Reignite the Spark of Novelty:** Routine and familiarity can sometimes dull the passion in a relationship. By introducing new activities and exploring different aspects of your sexuality, you can bring novelty and variety back into your sex life.

- **Build a Stronger Emotional Connection:** Sexual satisfaction and emotional connection are deeply intertwined. By improving your sexual communication, you also strengthen your overall emotional intimacy, leading to a more secure and harmonious relationship.

Your Erotic Menu is about creating a shared language of desire, curiosity, and respect that enhances every aspect of your life together. Through this course, you'll not only discover new ways to connect physically but also develop the emotional and communicative tools necessary to maintain a passionate relationship.

My Gift to You.

As a special gift for purchasing *The Turned-On Couple*, I'd like to offer you **exclusive access to *Your Erotic Menu*.**

Click on the link, or copy and paste it into your browser to gain access to this online program. I promise, your date nights will never be the same!

https://corinnefarago.com/youreroticmenu/

Is Relationship and Intimacy Coaching Right For You?

> *Your task is not to seek for love, but merely to seek and find all the barriers within yourself that you have built against it.*
>
> — Rumi

As most turned-on couples will tell you, good relationships require *work*.

But don't recoil! The work required is *good* work. It doesn't involve suffering battles, betraying values, or crossing boundaries. *Good* work means exploring our beliefs, shifting our perspectives, and expanding our understanding of what makes a great relationship!

As a relationship and intimacy coach, I view the coaching process as an education in how to love well — emotionally, erotically, and spiritually.

I look at relationship and intimacy coaching as having four developmental phases:

1. **The puzzle:** In the first phase of coaching I encourage couples to see their relationship as a third entity to be nurtured and

understood. This third entity is made up of both partner's history, emotional capacity, childhood wounds, goals and desires. In this stage of coaching I help couples view each individual piece as part of their shared relationship puzzle.

2. **The schooling:** In the second phase of coaching couples learn how to acquire the tools that are geared to their unique dynamic. These tools will help them through the challenging times that necessarily arise and bring them back into a secure connection built on trust and communication.

3. **The laboratory:** In the third phase of coaching couples can now begin to experiment with their new skills as if the relationship were a laboratory. Like scientists, couples explore new ways of communicating and connecting, looking for what works best for their dynamic. With each successful experiment they learn how to create a stable and secure foundation from which to grow and explore as a team.

4. **The practice:** In the fourth phase of coaching couples learn to commit to their new skills as a form of a personal practice. I say *personal* because it all comes back to the individuals and their capacity to keep turning back to love in the face of challenge or disappointment. Successful couples aren't challenge-free – they're just adept at nurturing their relationship, tending to its needs, and using the tools they've gathered to grow together emotionally and erotically.

Every one of these four phases has its risks and rewards that show us where we can grow more. Striving to love and be loved is part of our human experience. We'll never be perfect at it. In my opinion, learning how to love is our greatest lesson in life! We never arrive at the finish line and the learning never stops.

In a sense, an intimate relationship is your opportunity to learn, to fall down, to feel pain (and sometimes cause pain), to forgive and be forgiven, and to learn to give generously and receive graciously.

The practice of living in a thriving relationship is, in my opinion, the graduate school of being human.

So, when a couple comes to me because they've stopped having sex, or they fight too much, or they just know things could be better, I ask them if they're in a relationship to be satisfied by their partner or to grow and learn about themselves. Thework lies in honest self-reflection, acknowledgment of your own shortcomings, and the ability to step back into connection with an open and vulnerable heart. I tell them that's where the *real* work and the *real* rewards are found.

Relationship and intimacy coaching requires you to do this good work as a *team*. Couples learn to peel back the layers of obstruction that hold them back from deeper intimacy. They embrace the risks knowing the rewards will follow. They come to view their desire for coaching not as a sign of failure but as an opportunity to deepen their commitment to self-awareness, self-acceptance, and honest communication.

If after reading this book, you find yourself interested in private coaching, your first and most important step is setting up a Discovery Call with me here to learn more. https://calendly.com/corinnefarago/discovery-call

With love, passion and pleasure,
Corinne
corinne@corinnefarago.com

Index

www.ingramcontent.com/pod-product-compliance
Lightning Source LLC
Chambersburg PA
CBHW030400130626
46549CB00004B/1574